The Art of Cake Pops

The Art of Cake Pops

75 Dangerously Delicious Designs

Noel Muniz

Skyhorse Publishing

Skyhorse Publishing books may be purchased in bulk at special discounts for sales promotion, corporate gifts, fund-raising, or educational purposes. Special editions can also be created to specifications. For details, contact the Special Sales Department, Skyhorse Publishing, 307 West 36th Street, 11th Floor, New York, NY 10018 or info@skyhorsepublishing.com.

Skyhorse® and Skyhorse Publishing® are registered trademarks of Skyhorse Publishing, Inc.®, a Delaware corporation.

www.skyhorsepublishing.com

10 9 8 7 6 5 4 3 2 1

Library of Congress Cataloging-in-Publication Data is available on file.

ISBN: 978-1-62087-578-0

Printed in China

For my grandmother, Luz Pantoja.

Further dedicated to all the wonderful people who have supported The Cake Poppery over the years. This book is especially for you.

Contents

Getting Started

Cake Pop Basics

Cake pops are as much a science as they are an art form. Understanding the basic techniques will help you better understand the art of cake pops. It takes time and practice to master the craft of cake popping, but with a little patience and planning, you too can be making them like a professional. Every single step in the process of making cake pops will affect the overall outcome. Skipping a step or not properly planning ahead can cause a domino effect that will lead to less than desirable results.

The first and most important step in making cake pops is baking the cake. The cake is the foundation of a successful cake pop–making experience. The ideal cake for cake pops should be somewhat dense with some body to it and should be on the drier side. The cake should be slightly moist but not as moist as a traditional box cake, as you still want it to crumble. If you are making a cake from scratch, avoid any light and airy cakes, like angel food or sponge cake.

Ideally you want to bake the cake the night before and let it fully cool overnight. Not only

does that ensure you have a fully cooled cake, it allows the cake to dry up slightly, which is beneficial if you created a light and moist cake. The lower the moisture content the better, as it allows you more control with the texture when the binder is added. By not allowing the cake to fully cool and dry slightly when mixed with a binder, the cake will have a spongy texture and will not have as big of a pronounced flavor profile, as the binder gives the cake most of its flavor.

Although you might be under the impression you need to use frosting, it is not a necessary ingredient. Most boxed cakes will bind together without the use of frosting. If your cake is high in moisture it is best to opt out of adding it, but the flavor will be lacking. The use of frosting with a highly moist cake creates a variety of issues. When combined, the cake will be too soft and moist to roll into a perfect ball. The cake won't maintain its shape when rolled and will have the tendency to fall off the sticks when being dipped. It will also have a gummy texture.

If you opt out of using frosting or any binder, the best way to bind the cake is with a food processor. The food processor will blend it together until it is smooth; however, it will not create crumbs and will be creamier in texture than what you would normally get when mixing with a stand mixer or with your hands. When opting out of a binder, it is easier to bind your cakes while still warm. The heat from a warm cake will supply moisture for the cake without the use of an additional binder.

Now, if you plan on using homemade cake or cakes with a much lower moisture content, you will need a binder. Any liquid, frosting, or edible paste will do. You can use frosting, peanut butter, marshmallow fluff, fruit purée, any jam of your liking, and even water or juice if needed.

To crumble the cake, start off mixing it with the paddle attachment on a stand mixer without any frosting. Keep the mixer on low speed and allow the cake to fully crumble. When the crumbs look like sand, slowly add spoonfuls of the frosting or binder one at a time. As the cake is mixed with the binder, it will start to form tighter crumbs and will eventually come together into a tight dough like mixture. Once it starts to pull away from the sides of the mixer, it is ready. Depending on the cake, sometimes you will have to stop the mixer and test it for consistency after each addition of the binder. Some cakes will never form a tight crumb and will still look dry even if a binder is added, so you will have to test it.

To test if the cake is ready, knead it a few times on a countertop and roll some of the cake mixture in your hands. If it falls apart, you need to add more of the binder. The cake is ready once it holds its shape when rolled, and should be firm in texture. A three-to-one ratio is a good guide to go by when using a homemade cake. If you are using nine ounces of cake, you can expect to use at least three ounces of frosting. Always start off with less frosting than expected. You can always add more if needed.

Once you are ready to roll the balls, hand weigh each one to a one-ounce portion. A one-ounce cake ball will yield a pop that can be consumed in about two bites and is about one-and-a-half inches in diameter, the perfect size for a single person to enjoy. Place the dough in the palm of your hands while applying pressure and rotate your hands in a circular motion. As it starts to form a ball, gently relieve the pressure while maintaining the circular motion until your palms are barely touching it. If you end up with a rounded diamond shape, your cake is too moist. If you are working with a very firm, dense cake, moisten your hands to help with the rolling process. During this process you will need to clean your hands, as the cake residue will build up.

Once you have completed rolling all the balls, chill them slightly in the fridge if needed. While the cake balls are chilling, prepare the chocolate for dipping. A pound of chocolate will cover around two dozen cake pops. When melting chocolate, start off with melting only 75 percent of the chocolate you plan on using. Melt the chocolate in the microwave for thirty seconds and stir when finished. After the first thirty seconds, continue to melt in fifteen-second intervals,

stirring after every trip to prevent overcooking. Once the majority of the chocolate has melted, add the remaining chocolate and mix it together. Let it sit for a bit, as the residual heat will soften the chocolate and allow it to cool slightly so that it doesn't overheat. Melt for an additional fifteen seconds to remove any final lumps.

When the chocolate is ready and fully melted, dip the tips of the lollipop sticks into the chocolate and insert them halfway into the cake balls; allow to set before dipping. The chocolate will act as glue and keep the pop on the stick. You can wipe away the excess chocolate that pools up underneath the cake if desired. That ring of chocolate will also prevent the pop from changing position while tapping off any excess chocolate left there. It will also prevent the cake from sliding down the stick after being dipped. After all the sticks have been inserted into the pops, it is time to thin down the chocolate if it is too thick.

The chocolate should be fluid enough to coat a spoon without the edges of the metal showing through the chocolate. If you can see the metal of the spoon after being coated, your chocolate is too thin. If the chocolate clings to the spoon in an uneven manner, the chocolate is too thick and will have to be thinned down. The chocolate should fall in a smooth, steady stream when ready for dipping.

After the chocolate has reached the desired consistency, test the chocolate's finish. Dip the spoon into the chocolate and allow it to set. This will allow you to see the outcome of the chocolate and if there are any issues with discoloration or pitting. The chocolate should ideally be glossy or matte in color, depending on the brand. If there

are a bunch of white spots, the chocolate has bloomed, which is often a result of improper storage. There is no way to fix blooming once it has happened. Blooming can sometimes be masked with the use of a large amount of candy color added to the melted chocolate. If the chocolate dries with a streaky finish, the chocolate was not stirred

enough. The streaking is caused by the chocolate drying at different rates.

After the chocolate has been thinned down and the finish has been tested, you are ready to dip the pops. Make sure the chocolate on the sticks has fully hardened and that the balls are not cold. If the balls are cold the chocolate coating on the pops will crack. In a swift, steady motion, dunk the pop in the chocolate and pull it right out. Position it at an angle over your dipping vessel and gently shake off any excess chocolate. When you notice the amount falling off begins to decrease, gently tap the pop edge of your vessel while rotating it to ensure an even coat and remove any final excess. Place in a Styrofoam or wooden stand to dry, and you are ready to decorate.

Pop Tops • • • • • • • • • • • • • • • • • • •

Pop tops, cake truffles, or, if you prefer, plain old cake balls are often not approached with the same creativity as cake pops due to the difficulty in achieving a proper coating. Unlike a cake pop's stick, which allows for easy dipping, a cake ball is on its own. If you ever made cake balls before, you know how challenging it can be to make a pretty cake ball, especially one with a custom design. But any pop, regardless of shape or design, can technically become a cake ball. All you have to do is create the design you want as a cake pop. Once it is hard and fully decorated, cut the chocolate with a knife around the lollipop stick and twist it to gently remove it from the pop without damaging the design. Next, take the pop top to a heated pan on the stove. Place the hole flat on the pan and move in a circular pattern to melt the chocolate and cover the hole. Place on a silicone mat to cool and you have a foolproof, flawless custom cake ball.

Another more challenging method is using a fork and knife. Place the cake ball at the edge of your fork and fully submerge it into the melted chocolate. You can also spoon the chocolate over

the cake. Gently tap off all the extra chocolate and use the knife to slide the cake ball onto your silicone mat to cool.

7

The last possible method for cake balls is to chill them ahead of time. Prepare the chocolate and insert a toothpick into your cake ball, dip it, and treat it as a cake pop. Once you remove the excess chocolate, transfer it to your silicone mat and let cool. Once it is fully cool, remove the toothpick and hide the hole it created with a drizzle of chocolate.

To prevent the silicone mat from leaving exposed cake at the bottom of cake balls, chill the sheet pan so the chocolate will harden as soon as the balls are placed on it. You can also pipe a chocolate dot on a silicone mat and place the balls on top to seal up the cake or pipe chocolate onto the bottoms after being dipped.

Decorating Cake Pops • • • • •

Cake pops are edible art on a stick and are as cute as they are delicious. They may seem daunting to make for someone just starting out, as they offer endless possibilities. The only limit is your imagination! You can decorate cake pops with a variety of edible items, including sprinkles, cookies, candies, frosting, and chocolate. Cake pop decorating combines two of the most common pastry art forms: cake and sugar cookie decorating.

When creating a cake pop, you are essentially making a mini, scaled down cake. You should approach each cake pop as if it were both a cake and a sugar cookie. Focus on creating the basic shape and structure as if you were creating a cake, but treat the decor as if it were a sugar cookie.

You have many options when it comes to decorating cake pops. You can create designs and features with sprinkles or candies, or pipe or draw on all the details. Using candies and sprinkles allows you to create all sorts of designs and patterns. Sprinkles are wonderful to use to create small details, especially if you are not used to piping.

If you cannot find specific sprinkles, you can also pipe on all the details with melted chocolate or royal icing.

Sprinkles can be attached to cake pops while the chocolate is both wet and dry. The easiest way to transfer a sprinkle to a pop without leaving fingerprints is with tweezers or a toothpick. If the sprinkle you want to attach is flat, tap the tip of a toothpick on the surface of the sprinkles. Since sprinkles are porous, the tip will get stuck to the sprinkle, allowing for easy adhering to the pop.

If you are attaching sprinkles when wet, make sure they are not heavy so they don't fall and slide down the pop. If needed, allow the chocolate to cool a bit before attaching them while wet. Attaching them while wet will secure the candies or sprinkles into place so they cannot move or fall off, which is beneficial if you need to ship them. If you want to attach the sprinkles or candies once the chocolate has hardened, all you need to do is add small dots of melted chocolate with a toothpick, place the sprinkles or candies on top, and allow to set.

It can be hard to add really fine details to the pops using only sprinkles, and that is where edible markers, chocolate, and royal icing come into play. Using edible markers, you can draw any designs you wish, but they can be tricky to use as they can dig up the chocolate. For best results, store the markers tip-side down in the fridge and chill the pops before using the marker on them. Make sure the brand you purchase will write on chocolate, as most edible markers are not designed for doing this.

If you want to avoid using markers, you can pipe on all the details with chocolate or royal icing. Piping is the preferred decorating method to use because it is inexpensive, less time consuming, and uses the same chocolate as dipping. Chocolate details, unlike sprinkles, will not take away from the cake pops' texture. When piping chocolate, you need to make sure the chocolate is fluid and not too thick so that you have control over it. Consistency is key when using chocolate for decorating, just as when using royal icing when decorating sugar cookies.

There are three main consistencies to use when working with chocolate for piping. First is really fluid chocolate; with this consistency the chocolate should fall back into itself and not hold any shape whatsoever. This is perfect for flooding, as when creating the faces for a monkey cake pop. Using a really fluid-consistency chocolate is challenging for fine lines and details, for which you will want to use a medium-consistency chocolate. A medium consistency will slightly hold its shape. If you pipe it into a pile, the chocolate will slightly collapse on itself, but the individual lines of chocolate will be noticeable. Another consistency to use is a thick chocolate, which maintains shape after being piped and won't collapse on itself. You really want to use a thick consistency when creating textures like frosting, fur, or grass. The thick chocolate works wonders for piping a border on a cake or creating a grass skirt or even vines.

To pipe chocolate, melt it in a small plastic bag and snip the corner off of it. Try to snip off a small corner because the smaller the hole you cut the better it controls the thickness of your line. You can adjust the size of your lines with the size of the hole. When piping details on a pop, use a plastic bag filled with rice to keep the pop stationary for better control.

Piping chocolate does require a steady hand, and if you are having trouble getting used to it you can use royal icing instead. Use royal icing in a piping bag fitted with a number 1, number 2, or number 3 piping tip, depending on the desired thickness. Royal icing is more forgiving as you can easily wipe away any mistakes you make, unlike chocolate. Using a medium-consistency icing will give you the best control. If using royal icing, you should never bag the pops until it has fully hardened.

To practice piping details, on a sheet of paper trace the outline of various small cookie cutters. Place that sheet underneath wax paper and, using either chocolate or royal icing, practice decorating and piping in the small area to get used to working on a small surface.

Now, when making cake pops you do not have to focus on only doing custom shapes or designs. You can quickly and easily accent pops by topping round pops with drizzles, or sprinkles, or using chocolate molds to match your event theme. Using fondant is wonderful to create simple and effortless accents for pops.

Homemade vs. Boxed Cake ● ● ● ● ● ● ● ● ● ● ● ● ● ● ●

There is often a lot of discussion whether to use boxed cake mix or make a cake from scratch. Many people who are just entering the world of cake pops tend to use boxed cake mix because of how simple it is to prepare. The biggest benefit of using a mix is time. Most box cakes require as little as two to three ingredients, which are typically pantry staples. A homemade cake tends to be much more complicated and requires as many as six to seven ingredients, many of which you don't keep on hand all the time.

When it comes to shaping the cake into different designs it is easier to do with cake from a mix due to its really high moisture content. Many boxed mixes, after being baked, don't require much, if any, frosting. Boxed cake mixes also don't crumble, leaving them with a creamy texture, which allows the cake to be easily manipulated into various shapes.

But a huge drawback of a boxed mix is the texture and density. Since many boxed mixes produce highly moist cakes, when the cake is crumbled and mixed together you end up with a really light and soft filling. If you are not careful, you can easily add too much frosting and end up with a mushy mess. Although that soft filling is great for sculpting, a lot of people do not like the texture. If you are going to use a box cake you should allow it plenty of time to dry and cool down after baking. You should also limit or scale back the liquid ingredients in the recipe. Try adding less oil or water than required and avoid purchasing cakes with pudding in the mix.

Homemade cakes tend to be drier than boxed mixes, but they will yield cake pops with much better texture. Using a drier cake allows you more control in the finished product and gives you the chance to use various flavored binders to enhance the flavor of the pop. Cake pops made from scratch tend to have a dense, cake-like texture and crumble easily. The flavor is often bolder and more pronounced. Working with a homemade cake does take some time to get used to. Failing to add the proper amount of frosting will yield balls that will crumble in your hands while rolling.

In the end it comes down to personal preference. Box cakes are simple to make and easier to sculpt, whereas a homemade cake has a more pronounced flavor and maintains its shape better. If you plan ahead, go with the homemade cake for better flavor and texture, but if you are in a bind you can use a boxed mix cake.

Types of Chocolate • • • • • • • •

The type of chocolate you use can make or break your cake pop experience when making them for the first time. It is the most important aspect of cake pops. There are many options available on the market, which can make the whole process overwhelming. Currently, the most common types of chocolate stores carry fall into three categories. First you have candy melts, also known as confectionery wafers, which come as round, colored disks, generally in one-pound bags. The second type available is almond bark, which comes in the form of big bars weighing more than a pound. Lastly, you have common baking chocolate, like chocolate chips and bars. They are generally sold in bags or bars weighing around twelve ounces for bags or four to six ounces for bars.

Candy melts are the most popular type used for cake pops since they do not need to be tempered and, when dried, will be much harder and durable than a regular baking chocolate will be. They come pre-colored so you are limited in color choices, but you can always add candy color or any oil-based food color to brighten them up. Candy melts can be found in most craft and hobby stores, and online. Each brand of candy melts has a different consistency when melted, and it is important to know that difference before dipping your cake pops. Some brands work better than others do in specific weather and environments. You want to use a brand that best fits where you live. Try to use a chocolate that falls off of your spoon in a silky smooth stream when melted. Most brands do require thinning down to achieve a fluid chocolate that is acceptable for dipping.

Candy melts can sometimes overcook in the microwave. Because of their quarter-sized disk shape, the chocolate is more exposed to the heat of the microwave, which can make chocolate too thick for dipping. Another common issue is the chocolate blooming during transit from factory to store. When the chocolate is stored in conditions over seventy-five degrees, some of the fat becomes visible on the surface, which is seen as white spots once it hardens. It is a purely cosmetic issue and does not affect the flavor.

Almond bark is the second most popular choice and can only be found in vanilla or chocolate. Almond bark works just as wonderful as candy melts do; nearly all brands on the market tend to melt silky smooth with no need to be thinned down. They also give you more control with color designs since you are working with a blank canvas. They come in brick form, which allows you to take as much or as little as needed. What is also great about almond bark is that blooming is rare and mainly affects the smaller bars and disk types of chocolate. The brands of almond bark that include a melting tray typically melt the smoothest and are the best tasting. The only downside it that cheap almond bark can have a grainy feel and is not as sweet as candy melts are. If you like you can mix almond bark with candy melts.

Candy melts and almond bark are not, in fact, real chocolate. Chocolate has cocoa butter in it and requires tempering to provide a shine and snap to it. Tempering chocolate is the process of heating and cooling chocolate to control the crystallization of cocoa butter. Candy melts and almond bark have the cocoa butter replaced by another type of fat, traditionally vegetable oil, which allows you to skip the whole tempering process. In some areas and parts of the globe you cannot find almond bark or candy melts.

The last type of chocolate you can use is traditional baking chocolate. This is great if you are in

a bind since it is readily available at most stores. However, it tends to require much more work than the others since it requires tempering and costs more. In order to use any real chocolate it is best to temper it first. This process is needed to produce a firm, glossy chocolate with a good snap to it. To temper chocolate, start off by setting up a double boiler. Chop your chocolate and melt two-thirds of it in the double boiler, constantly stirring. Heat it until it reaches 110°F for milk or white chocolate, or 115°F for dark chocolate. Once it reaches the proper temperature, remove the bowl from the heat and add the remaining chocolate, stirring until the temperature drops back down to 80–82°F. Place the bowl back over the heat and reheat until you reach 86–88°F for milk and 88–89°F for dark chocolate. Once at the desired temperature, you are ready to dip.

If you are wondering whether you can use chocolate chips as the coating, the answer is yes and no. The majority of brands available on the market tend to have an additive in them that helps the chocolate maintain its shape at high temperatures. So by the time they finally melt smoothly the chocolate will have overheated and missed the proper tempering temperatures. You can technically use it, but it will never be as hard as candy melts or almond bark are and will be soft to the touch.

Coloring Chocolate

For the majority of the time when working with cake pops, you will have to make and mix custom colors. If the chocolate you are using is not pre-colored, you can color it on your own. There are two ways to color chocolate. The most popular way is with candy color, which is an oil-based food color. You can also use powdered food coloring. Do not use water-based color or gel color, as those will seize your chocolate and render it useless. Seizing occurs when liquid is added to chocolate while it is melted, which causes it to harden and become unable to melt again. Oil-based colors are great because they come in a wide variety of colors and are potent.

The only downside to candy color, besides its staining ability if spilled, is that specific colors tend to thicken the chocolate quickly. Colors like yellow, orange, blue, and green will make your chocolate too thick to dip into when added in large amounts. When dealing with a color like orange, it is best to use yellow as a base for the chocolate and add the orange to it. If the chocolate ends up too thick due to large amounts

of added color, thin it down with cooking oil. Another good thing about candy color is that a little goes a long way with some colors. A little drop of pink into white can give you a bright hot pink in seconds; the more used, the brighter the color gets. If you add too much of other colors— for example, red or black—they will alter the taste of the chocolate, giving you a bitter, metallic flavor.

The other option is powdered food color. It is recommended to blend powdered food color into oil before adding it to chocolate. This allows the chocolate to accept the color easier. The downside of powdered color is that it takes a lot more of it to color chocolate, and it's not as potent as its commercially available oil based; counterparts. You can find most colors as oil-based, however, neon and metallic colors are not sold in oil based form. If the color you need is not sold in an oil-based form, you can always boost the color after it has dried with petal or luster dust.

To add the color, dip a toothpick into the color then stir it in the chocolate. Doing it this way allows you to have better control of the color's intensity than if you poured it in a drop at a time. After you have successfully colored the chocolate, keep in mind some colors will intensify as they sit. You should allow the chocolate to sit after being colored to ensure you end up with the desired color. Make sure to fully stir in the color to avoid streaks on the pops.

If you need to use black for a pop, start off with dark chocolate as your base. Dark chocolate meant specifically for candy fountains works best because it is naturally fluid when melted. To achieve the right black, you can use black candy color with some purple added; the addition will intensify the black color of the chocolate. When wet, the chocolate will have a blackish purple hue to it, but once it dries it will be jet black. You can also mix red with black. If you don't have black candy color on hand you can use blue and purple with dark chocolate. Avoid using light colors like pink, yellow, or orange. The downside of using black for a cake pop is that it can stain your mouth if too much food color is added. If you are going to use black for cake pops, make it an accent color and not the base color.

Another popular color used in cake pops is a flesh tone. Creating a flesh-tone pop can be done in numerous ways. The first is with peanut butter melts. Melt the peanut butter–flavored candy melts and add white or milk chocolate as needed to achieve the proper skin tone desired. However, with the amount of peanut allergies nowadays, many people cannot use peanuts. You can also use butterscotch-flavored candy melts, but it is an acquired taste. The best bet for achieving a peach skin tone is mixing even portions of white, pink, and yellow candy melts. Add a few chips of regular chocolate to darken the flesh tone if needed. You can also start off with white chocolate as your base and add very small amounts of milk chocolate to it until you achieve the desired color.

Melting and Storing Chocolate ● ● ● ● ● ● ● ● ● ● ● ● ● ●

A key step in making cake pops is melting the chocolate. The first option is the double boiler method. Heat a pot with about an inch or two of water to a simmer and place a heat-proof bowl on top, so that it is being heated by the steam. Place the chocolate inside the bowl and slowly keep stirring until it is melted. The double boiler method is the safer of the two methods to use, but it is much more time consuming.

The other, more popular method is with a microwave. The microwave is the quickest method to use when melting chocolate. Pour 75 percent of the chocolate you plan on melting into a bowl and microwave it for thirty seconds. Once the thirty seconds are up, stir so the chocolate doesn't get unevenly cooked. Put it in for another fifteen seconds then continue melting the chocolate in fifteen-second intervals until smooth. Once smooth, add the remaining 25 percent of chocolate and stir. Let it rest on the counter for a few minutes to soften the newly added chocolate. (The reason to melt only 75 percent of the chocolate then add the remaining 25 percent is

so that the chocolate does not over heat. Adding the remaining 25 percent of the chocolate will cool it down, especially if it is close to becoming overcooked.) After the chocolate has softened, place it back in the microwave and heat until fully melted. If you have any stubborn lumps of chocolate that won't melt, you can use an immersion blender to break up those chunks or strain them out.

If the melted chocolate is thick and not fluid, it could be the brand, as some naturally melt into a thick consistency. Heating it up more will not make it any thinner. Too much time in the microwave will overheat it. Overheated chocolate will be slightly thick and appear cracked and separated. An easy way to tell if the chocolate is overheated is to scoop it up with a spoon and allow it to fall back into the bowl. When it falls back into

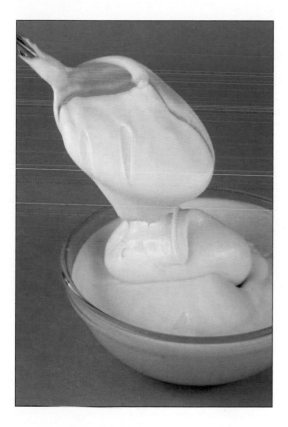

the bowl, the spoon will have layers of chocolate looking as if it cracked and separated.

If you feel that the chocolate is on the verge of becoming overcooked, add un-melted chocolate, which will help balance out the heat and cool it down. If you did overcook your chocolate, you can save it by thinning it down. Make sure the type of fat you use is waterless. Do not use butter or margarine, which contain water. Cooking oil, shortening, or paramount crystals all work perfectly fine. Avoid using olive oil, due to the taste it leaves behind, or nut oils, in case of allergies. Make sure to fully mix the fat into the chocolate before dipping, otherwise the pops will have a streaky finish.

A small amount of oil can go a long way. Start with less than a teaspoon and gradually add more until you reach the desired consistency. If you add too much oil it will weaken the chocolate and take much longer to set. Sometimes if you go overboard with the oil, it will not set and will remain soft to the touch. Your pops will also have a spotted texture once dried if too much oil was added. If you don't want to thin down the chocolate, the thick chocolate works wonders for creating details and accents for the pops.

When it comes to storing the chocolate, you want to keep it in a cool, dry place. Storing chocolate in a damp environment will cause the chocolate to bloom. After you have dipped all

your pops and you have finished with the chocolate, make sure to strain it in a fine mesh strainer. This removes crumbs and chocolate lumps that might be remaining, as well as any stray candies or sprinkles used in decorating. You have two main options for storing it. The most popular method is to store the chocolate in the containers that pre-made frosting comes in. Those containers are microwave safe, stackable, and easy to store. Use the ones with a clear lid so you can know which container has which color.

If you don't want to melt a whole container of chocolate, especially when you only need a little of one color, you can also pour the melted chocolate into small silicone molds. This allows you to pick and chose the amount needed instead of melting a large batch of chocolate. The difference between storing it in a container as a large mass and storing it in small molded shapes depends on when you melt it.

When you re-melt the chocolate, there are two typical outcomes. When you store your chocolate as a large block, it tends to melt much better than when storing as smaller blocks. Melting smaller chunks of chocolate exposes them to more heat and the consistency might become thick. But if you don't stir the large blocks of chocolate in the frosting containers, most of the heat ends up focused on the bottom, which causes the chocolate to crystallize. Once chocolate has crystallized, there is no saving it, even if you strain.

Chilling Before Dipping ● ● ● ●

Chilling your pops before dipping is a personal choice that should be made based off of the cake you use. If you are using a cake that is really soft with high moisture content, you should chill the pops before dipping so they retain their shape and stay on the stick. But if you use a dense cake, especially a homemade one, chilling is not needed. The main benefit of chilling the pops is they are firm when dipped and won't fall into the chocolate. Chilling is also beneficial when working in summer heat as it allows the pops to set much faster. But if your pops are too cold, the chocolate will set before it has the chance to evenly smooth out.

If you chill the cake mixture before rolling, it will make the cake easier to handle. You should also chill the cake mixture if you plan on using a cookie cutter as a mold so the cake will be firm and easier to push out from the cutter. If you are making cake balls or a cake pop where the stick will come up from the top, you can dip them chilled without worrying about them cracking; when they rest on a silicone mat or parchment paper, the bottom of the cake will be exposed, which will alleviate the pressure.

The main downside of chilling is the pops cracking. As the pops chill they will shrink slightly, so

when they start to return to room temperature the cake will expand and try to force its way out. The pressure will build up and cause the chocolate to crack. This can be a nightmare, especially after you have decorated your cake pops, and sometimes it can take up to thirty minutes before they crack. To avoid this, make sure that you let them come to room temperature before dipping and that your chocolate is cool to the touch. You can also experience cracking if you pipe on details or designs with chocolate that is too hot.

To fix cracked pops, you can either pipe melted chocolate into the crack to smooth it or you can double dip. If you are going to double dip the pops, allow the pops to rest before dipping so that the cake will shrink and close the gap created from the cracked chocolate.

Smooth Cake Pops ● ● ● ● ● ● ● ● ●

Achieving perfectly smooth pops takes time and practice, but with a few helpful tips you will be on your way. It all begins with the base. Remember that when you go to dip any pop, whether a round ball or a shape, the chocolate will cover every nook and cranny of the cake. If the ball of cake starts off lumpy or with cracks and creases in it, the end result will show that. So you have to make sure you have the correct cake consistency for rolling.

First make sure that you don't add too much frosting to the cake mixture. Always start to mix the cake without frosting, then slowly add frosting a little at a time until it binds together. The cake filling should be slightly stiff, like children's clay but pliable. The cake-to-frosting ratio that generally works is 3 to 1. If you add too much frosting or the cake is too moist to begin with, you will end up with mushy dough that won't maintain its shape. Remember, less is more when it comes to frosting. If it is too sticky, you can always add more cake to it or roll pops when the cake is chilled to achieve a smooth ball.

When working with a drier cake, a splash of water on your hands works wonders, especially when dealing with homemade cakes or altered boxed cakes. Both tend to be harder to roll and tend to crack if you don't have enough frosting. The outer crumb layer will loosen, which will make a smoother ball as it moves around in the palms of your hands.

If, when rolling, you keep getting rounded, cone-shaped ends on your ball, either your hands or the cake are too wet. To fix that, dry your hands and start over. Once you have a rounded ball, gently shape any minor imperfections on it with your fingertips to create an even sphere.

The last key step is to use fluid chocolate. If the chocolate is thick it, will be much harder to get a smoother looking pop and it will generally fall off the stick. To see if your chocolate is fluid enough, scoop some up with a spoon and let it fall back into your bowl. It should fall in a steady stream. If the chocolate is too thick and plops back into the bowl, you can adjust the consistency. Never dip the pops in chocolate that has been overheated, as the pops will not have a smooth finish.

When dipping the cake pops, make sure the chocolate is in a deep enough container so that the cake can be completely submerged. Fully submerge the pop into the chocolate, pull it up quickly, and hold it at a forty-five-degree angle and gently shake it side to side so that the chocolate from the top slides and falls off the bottom. After you have most of the chocolate off, gently tap it on the dipping vessel while rotating to remove all the excess chocolate and smooth it out.

When dipping a shaped pop, each pop will have a positive side and a negative side. The positive side is the presentation side and the back is the negative. Hold the pop so that the positive side faces you and tap your wrist with your free hand to tap off any excess chocolate to make sure you get a smooth finish. The back side will have what we call the drip line.

Drip lines are what forms when the chocolate falls back into the bowl, creating lines and ridges of chocolate on the pop. After the positive side is smooth and no more chocolate is falling into the bowl, flip the pop over with the negative side facing you and gently shake the pop from left to right, allowing the chocolate to smooth out on the back side of the pop to remove any drip lines.

Pops Falling Off During Dipping

If you find yourself with a batch of cake pops that keep falling off of the sticks while dipping, various things can be the cause. If the cake is too wet when you insert the stick, the chocolate will have nothing to cling on to. The moisture will create a barrier between the chocolate and cake, preventing it from sticking. Always make sure to use a cake that is not too moist before dipping.

Pops can also fall off and slide down the sticks if you don't let the chocolate that was inserted into the stick set before dipping. That chocolate acts as both glue and support for the cake and prevents it from falling off.

Another issue is pop weight. The ideal size is one ounce of cake filling. If you try making a pop that is over two ounces, the weight of the pop and chocolate will cause it to fall off. Sometimes if you push your stick too far up into the cake, the weight of the chocolate will cause the cake to slide and break after being dipped. Make sure to never stick it in further than half way.

Chocolate is another culprit. If you attempt to dip in chocolate that is too thick, the cake will fall off due to the weight of the chocolate. Always use a fluid chocolate when dipping.

Cookie Cutters as Molds ● ● ●

The novelty of cake pops is being able to turn cake into uniquely shaped edible art. Sometimes there are shapes we just cannot create by using our hands, and instead, you can use cookie cutters. Cookie cutters come in all shapes, designs, and sizes. They are a cake pop maker's best friend, as they allow you to achieve new and exciting shapes that were unachievable before.

Small cookie cutters, two inches or smaller in size, make for great molds, but removing the cake from them can be quite challenging if you are not prepared. If you have trouble removing the cake from a cookie cutter, keep a bowl of water next to you and place the cookie cutter inside. Lightly dampen your hands, remove the cutter from the water, and place on a flat surface. Stuff the cutter with cake and gently push the shape out from any sharp point. The water will act as a lubricant and allow it to easily slide out. Once removed, flip the shape over and lightly tap the surface of it with the palm of your hand to flatten out all the indentations you created while removing the shape. If you are having trouble with removing the cake, chilling the dough ahead of time makes this process easier.

Now that you have a shaped pop, inserting the stick can be troublesome depending on the thickness you created. If you insert the stick and notice cracks where it has gone through, pipe chocolate along the lines and smooth it over to add support to the shape. To avoid those cracks, hold the shape in the center with your fingers and gently insert the stick. The cracks will appear if the cake mixture is not moist enough.

When you create a shape by hand, all the edges are naturally round so the chocolate clings to it, but once you use a cookie cutter as a mold, you are left with sharp edges of cake that become visible after being dipped. To prevent this you can use a light color cake, smooth the edges, or double dip. To smooth out the edges, flatten all the sharp edges with your fingertips.

Double dipping your cake pops is a great method, as it hides all blemishes and cake from showing through, which gives you a more polished looking pop. If you are going to double dip your pops, make sure the chocolate is fluid and much thinner than you would normally use. If you don't thin down the chocolate, the second coat will be too heavy. They can also fall off the stick when drying so make sure your first coat of chocolate is thinner than the second coat.

Yellow Sticks ● ● ● ● ● ● ● ● ● ● ● ●

When making cake pops, you might find that some of the sticks begin to change color and become yellow shortly after being dipped. This is purely a cosmetic issue, not a sign that the pops have spoiled. The yellowing is the result of the moisture from the fat being absorbed into the paper of the sticks. This does not always happen but will occasionally, depending on the heat as well as the type of cake and frosting combo used.

The yellowing has a greater likelihood of happening if the cake is from a boxed mix. Not only do most boxed cakes have a higher moisture content, but also most have a higher fat content than homemade cakes, which tend to be drier and butter based. It is always best to seek out a butter based recipe or replace the fat in the cake with applesauce to prevent this.

The type of frosting you use is just as important as the type of cake that goes into your pops. If you are using a cream cheese frosting or a butter cream high in fat, it is only a matter of time before the sticks change color. Most homemade frostings require a lot of butter, and when left out in the heat they tend to separate, which allows the fat to seep into the lollipop sticks. To limit the yellowing of sticks, always try to pair a homemade cake with a canned frosting, which will limit the amount of fat.

If you have been making pops for a long time and just noticed this happening lately, keep the season in mind. The warmer the weather, the more likely and faster the yellowing will occur due to the fat being at a warmer, liquid state. There are two main ways to slow down or prevent this from happening. After you have finished decorating your pops, individually wrap them and place them in the fridge to make the fat stay in a solid form.

The other method to prevent this completely is pre-dipping all the sticks into melted chocolate, before making the pops. Let the chocolate harden, then once again dip the stick into melted chocolate and then your pops. This creates a barrier between the stick and cake that doesn't allow oil or fat to be absorbed into the stick. You could also use plastic sticks, but they are harder to find in stores and often require special online purchases. Another way to hide the yellowing is to dip the pop further into the chocolate, so that it is not visible.

There are going to be times while creating pops that you will notice them oozing a clear yellow liquid. That liquid is nothing more than the fat that hasn't been absorbed into the stick trying to escape. What happens is the pressure from the inside causes the fat to seep out of any tiny exposed holes. It will always come out from the weak spots in the chocolate, anywhere there is an air bubble.

To prevent this, try not to stir the chocolate as much, and if you find yourself with a lot of air bubbles, you can gently shake them out. If needed, straining your chocolate through a metal sieve will also remove the air bubble. Air bubbles are often found in thicker chocolate. If you add some oil and stir, most air bubbles will disappear. When tapping off the excess chocolate, pop air bubbles ahead of time.

You can always double dip the pops to prevent air bubbles from forming. If you find yourself with a pop that has started to leak oil, just set it aside and wait until this stops. Eventually the internal pressure will be relieved and the fat will stop coming out. Wipe the grease and cover the hole with melted chocolate. Remove the excess and set aside to dry.

Heat and Humidity · · · · · · · · ·

Whether you are a seasoned pro or someone just starting out, you know how much a hassle summer and warm weather can be. In the summer, all the elements are against you and making cake pops can be quite challenging. Not only do you have to deal with the high temperatures, you also have to deal with humidity and dry heat, which will completely alter the consistency of the chocolate you are using.

Some types of chocolate will fare better in heat and humidity. Almond barks will melt the same way as they did during the cooler months. Since they are sold in a thick bar form, the heat has less surface area to soften the chocolate. However, due to candy melts' shape and size, it takes a lot less time for the heat to soften the chips. If you touch one during the summer it will be soft and will bend instead of snapping when you try to break it in half. Candy melts do not fare well in summer heat, so many stores will stop carrying them from June to October.

If you don't treat the chocolate it will melt down into a thick paste-like texture. To fix that and return it to normal consistency you will have to firm up the chocolate and restore its snap. To do so, place it in the freezer for a few minutes until it is hard again and breaks with a clean smooth snap in half. Make sure to melt it right away before it has the chance to soften again after being removed from the freezer. If it sweats, then the chocolate will seize, or turn into a lumpy consistency, and be ruined.

The other issue with summer heat is the time it takes to harden the chocolate. The pops will lose the glossy shine that they have from being freshly dipped and go into the normal matte finish without hardening. If you live in an area where it is hot during the day and cold at night, the best time to dip your pops would be at night so the cold air can harden the pops. If it is hot both day and night, you have two options. Dip your pops in an air-conditioned room or, after dipping, place them in the fridge to harden and set. However, taking them to the fridge after being dipped can cause the chocolate to bloom.

The heat will also affect the finish that your pops will have. Since it takes so long for the pops to set in heat, you will end up with a finish that looks more like leather and that may also spot. Spotting occurs when air bubbles collapse and form small, dark-colored indentations. Spotting is most common if pops are left out in warm weather for a long period of time. Store the pops in the fridge or a cold environment to prevent this.

Preparing Pops Ahead of Time ● ● ● ● ● ● ● ● ● ● ●

Preparing a large amount of cake pops can seem like a daunting task, but all it takes is a little bit of planning and organization. Contrary to belief, a pop does not taste fresher if it was made on the same day. Once the cake has been dipped, it will not dry out or go stale. In fact, some flavors taste better when made two to three days ahead of time. Cake pops can last up to two weeks depending on flavors and fillings. If you use fresh fruit, they will remain good only for a few days. But as long as the pops do not have any perishable ingredients, they will last well over a week.

There are two different ways to approach the production of a large number of cake pops if you are working with limited time. Some people prefer to bake the cake, roll the balls, and freeze the cake balls until they are needed. To freeze the un-dipped balls, line a sheet pan with parchment paper and fill up the pan. Freeze the cake balls for a few hours until firm, then place them in an airtight container or in a plastic bag and keep frozen until ready to use. The only downside of freezing the cake balls is they do tend to dry out and lose flavor if left in the freezer for a long period of time.

The preferred method to keep the cake as fresh and flavorful as possible is to bake the cake the night before you plan on using it. This allows the cake not only to cool down completely before being mixed with the frosting, but also allows any excess moisture to dry out, giving you more control over the texture. The following morning, blend the cake with the frosting, place the cake filling in an airtight container or plastic bag, and refrigerate until ready to use. This is a good method to utilize if your cake is really dry because it gives the cake and frosting time to fuse. You can keep the cake filling in the fridge up to a week before it needs to be rolled. The cake you need is ready to go, and large orders will be a breeze.

Once the cake is dipped into chocolate, you can freeze the pops, but should do so with caution as the chocolate can discolor and will sweat when removed from the freezer. It is best to only freeze leftover pops. To store your decorated pops, individually wrap each pop and place them in an airtight container in the fridge to prolong their freshness for upwards of two weeks.

Fundamental Cake Pop Supplies

Any cake pop artist is only as good as the tools he or she owns. Making cake pops does not require many tools, but there are certain items that every cake pop artist should use when making pops. Plenty of fantastic designs can be made with the bare minimum, but with the help of a few specialty baking items, ordinary pops can be turned into extraordinary works of art. There are so many useful items sold in stores that can help you become a better artist. Never limit yourself to just the baking supply aisles in craft stores. You can find many molds and cutters in the jewelry and clay sections too. Here are some of the most important and versatile tools to help take your pops to the next level.

Stand mixer Although a stand mixer is not necessary, it makes binding the cake with the frosting a breeze. You can mix your cake with frosting by hand but it is messy and more time consuming. Using a stand mixer is a cleaner and faster method that perfectly blends the two together without leaving behind any large chunks of cake.

Digital scale A digital scale is your best friend when making cake pops. It allows you to make sure all your pops are the same exact size and weight. By hand-weighing the pops on a digital scale, you are able to produce much more consistent results. The ideal weight for a cake pop is one ounce of cake filling; it is the perfect serving size and surface area for decorating.

Cookie cutters Cookie cutters are wonderful tools to utilize. They come in all sorts of sizes and designs and can be used in various ways. The small-sized cookie cutters allow you to create shapes that would have been otherwise impossible. Using them as a mold allows you to create pops with sharper edges and obscure shapes that are not achievable through hand sculpting. The ideal size cutters to use are two inches and smaller; anything larger and the pops will be too heavy to dip. Look for nesting cookie cutter sets typically meant for fondant, as those are the perfect size to use as a mold.

Floral gum paste cutter sets

A floral gum paste set can be vastly utilized in cake pops, not only for making flowers, but as accents for other pops. A small rose petal cutter can be used for creating the ear of a mouse or the wing of a bird. Larger petals can create bunny ears, or a daisy can become a collar for clown pops.

Molds

Whether they are chocolate or fondant molds, they are great to have on hand to add little details to cake pops. They are perfect to utilize when you want to add small details like bows, flowers, buttons, or seashells without the use of fondant. Using a mold is a quick way to create accent pops that take little effort and time.

Pasta machine

A pasta machine is great to use when rolling out fondant. It allows you to roll the fondant to the same thickness and ensure uniformity when working in large volumes. It also ensures everything dries at the same rate. Use it on the thinnest thickness to roll out fondant paper-thin for the skirts or ruffles of dress cake pops.

Paintbrushes

Every cake pop artist should have at least two sets of paintbrushes in various widths and sizes. Stiff- and soft-bristle sets are a must-have. The stiff-bristle paintbrushes come in handy when making textures like fur, grass, or wood grains, as well as adding textured flowers using the brush embroidery technique. You want to use the soft brushes when adding or using luster or petal dust, as well as when painting details onto the pops. With a soft-bristle brush you can add rosy cheeks to babies and add highlights to different shapes. An airbrushed effect can also be achieved with a soft-bristled paintbrush and petal dust.

Plastic bags

Plastic bags make wonderful piping bags for adding small details to cake pops. Fill them with chocolate and snip off a corner to pipe on eyes, add details to flowers, or even add a pacifier to a baby pop. Make sure to use microwave-safe bags so that the chocolate can be stored and reused in them. The 3 x 5 inch poly bags sold to cover cake pops are the ideal bags to use, as they hold up well to the heat of a microwave and are not too thin.

Fondant

A box of fondant should always be kept in your pantry for cake pops. You can use it for everything from flowers to ears and to add texture to your pops. It is best used underneath chocolate to add details and as support for when you need something stable enough to handle the weight of the chocolate. It is also great to create depth in your pops and accents to go on top. Fondant is an under-utilized aspect of cake pops due to the fact many people do not like the taste of commercial fondant. If you dislike the taste, try making marshmallow fondant (on page 47). It complements many cake pop flavors, especially chocolate cake; however, it does not dry as hard as traditional fondant does.

Royal icing

Although chocolate is very versatile and many effects can be achieved with it, there are certain things chocolate cannot convey properly, and that is where royal icing comes into play. It can convey fluffiness and lightness when creating clouds, dollops of whipped cream, or icing on a cake. If you don't want to pipe details with chocolate and want better control, use royal icing with a #1 or #2 piping tip to create fine lines and details.

Edible markers

Edible markers are useful for fine lines and to add details on everything from chocolate to fondant. Not all edible markers will write on chocolate, so you will need to read the package; most can only write on fondant and royal icing. Always buy food-safe edible markers. Just because a marker is non-toxic does not mean it should be consumed. When storing your markers make sure to keep them tip-side down in the fridge to prevent the tips from drying out. If you have trouble getting them to write, chill your pops after being dipped, especially if you thin down your chocolate with oil, so the marker doesn't pull up the chocolate and clog the tip.

Luster and petal dust

These are available in a wide variety of colors and have many uses. Try using them dry and dust them on pops to add highlights and create shading on shaped pops. The use of luster dust will give your pops a pearlized effect and allow them to sparkle in sunlight, giving them a glittering look that is perfect for a princess party or girls' night out. They can also be used for painting on details when mixed with lemon juice or vodka.

Sprinkles

You can never own too many sprinkles. Sprinkles are available in all sorts of colors and designs. There is a sprinkle for every holiday and special occasion on the market. They are vastly used in the making of cake pops. You can use them underneath chocolate to add depth to your pops or on top as decorations. Sugar pearls are great for noses, confetti sprinkles for eyes, and hearts for bows and ears.

Candy

Candies are the most versatile edible item to use in cake pops. Disk-shaped candies make great ears for bears, while sphere-shaped candies are perfect for noses, and string candy can be used for handles and hair when needed. If you are using hard candies or too many sprinkles they can take away from the texture and flavor of the cake pops. Always make it known what candies are used on your cake pops to avoid choking. There is nothing worse than biting into a cake pop expecting a lush, dense cake filling only to be greeted by a rock-hard piece of candy.

Preparing the Cake

Banana Cake •••••••••••••••••

Yield: 17 ounces

Ingredients

- ¾ cup flour
- ½ teaspoon of cinnamon
- ½ teaspoon baking soda
- 5 tablespoons butter, room temperature
- ¾ cup white sugar
- 1 egg, room temperature
- ¾ cup of mashed ripe bananas
- 1 teaspoon vanilla
- ¼ cup milk

1. Preheat oven to 350°F (175°C). Grease and flour a 9 x 9 inch cake pan.

2. Sift together the flour, baking soda, and cinnamon. Set aside.

3. In a large bowl, cream together the butter and sugar. Beat in the egg and vanilla until combined, then beat in the mashed bananas.

4. Add the flour mixture, scraping down the sides if needed, and mix until combined.

5. Add the milk and beat until smooth. Pour the batter into the prepared pan.

6. Bake in the preheated oven for twenty to thirty minutes, or until top springs back when lightly touched.

7. Allow to fully cool before crumbling for cake balls.

Chocolate Cake • • • • • • • • • • •

Yield: 27 ounces

Ingredients

- 1½ cups flour
- 1 teaspoon baking soda
- ¼ teaspoon baking powder
- ½ cup cocoa powder
- ½ cup butter, room temperature
- 1 cup white sugar
- 2 eggs, room temperature
- 1 teaspoon vanilla
- ¾ cup strongly brewed coffee

1. Preheat oven to 350°F (175°C). Grease and flour a 9 x 13 inch cake pan.

2. Sift together the flour, cocoa powder, baking soda, and baking powder. Set aside.

3. In a large bowl, cream together the butter and sugar. Beat in the eggs one at a time and add vanilla until combined.

4. Alternate adding the flour mixture and strongly brewed coffee, scraping down the sides if needed, and mix until combined.

5. Bake for twenty to thirty minutes, or until top springs back when lightly touched.

6. Allow to fully cool before crumbling for cake balls.

Lemon Cake • • • • • • • • • • • • •

Yield: 18 ounces

Ingredients

- 1 cup flour
- 1 teaspoon baking powder
- ½ cup of butter, room temperature
- ¾ cup white sugar
- 2 eggs, room temperature
- 1 teaspoon vanilla
- 1½ teaspoons finely grated lemon zest
- ½ cup fresh-squeezed lemon juice

1. Preheat oven to 350°F (175°C). Grease and flour a 9 x 9 inch cake pan.

2. Sift together the flour and baking powder. Set aside.

3. In a large bowl, cream together the butter and sugar. Beat in the eggs one at a time until combined, then beat in the vanilla and lemon zest.

4. Alternate adding the flour mixture and lemon juice, scraping down the sides if needed, and mix until combined.

5. Bake in the preheated oven for twenty to thirty minutes, or until top springs back when lightly touched.

6. Allow to fully cool before crumbling for cake balls.

Note

If you prefer a more subtle lemon flavor, replace half of the lemon juice with water.

Strawberry Cake • • • • • • • • • • •

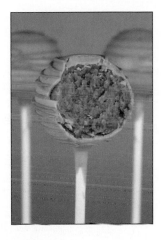

Yield: 30 ounces

Ingredients

- 1½ cups flour
- 1 teaspoon baking powder
- 3-ounce package of strawberry-flavored gelatin
- ¾ cup of butter, room temperature
- 1¼ cups white sugar
- 2 eggs, room temperature
- 1 teaspoon vanilla
- 1¼ cups of strawberry puree made from frozen strawberries

1. Preheat oven to 350°F (175°C). Grease and flour a 9 x 13 inch cake pan.

2. Sift together the flour, baking soda, and gelatin. Set aside.

3. In a large bowl, cream together the butter and sugar. Beat in the eggs one at a time until combined, then beat in the vanilla.

4. Alternate adding the flour mixture and the strawberry puree, scraping down the sides if needed, and mix until combined.

5. Bake in the preheated oven for twenty to thirty minutes, or until top springs back when lightly touched.

6. Allow to fully cool before crumbling for cake balls.

Yellow Cake

Yield: 27 ounces

Ingredients

- 1¾ cups flour
- 1½ teaspoons baking powder
- ¾ cup butter, chilled
- 1½ cups white sugar
- 8 egg yolks, chilled
- 1 teaspoon vanilla
- ½ cup milk, chilled

1. Preheat oven to 350°F (175°C). Grease and flour a 9 x 13 inch cake pan.

2. Sift together the flour and baking powder until there are no lumps. Set aside.

3. In a large bowl, cream together the butter and sugar. Add the egg yolks one at a time to the butter and sugar mixture. Stir in the vanilla and beat until combined.

4. Add the flour mixture in thirds, alternating with two additions of the milk, mixing just until combined. You will start and finish with the flour. Pour the batter into the prepared pan.

5. Bake in the preheated oven for twenty-five to thirty minutes, or until top springs back when lightly touched.

6. Allow to fully cool before crumbling for cake balls.

Marshmallow Fondant · · · · · ·

Ingredients

- 1 pound white mini marshmallows
- 2 tablespoons water
- 2 pounds powdered sugar
- ½ cup shortening

1. Grease a microwave-safe bowl with the shortening and melt the marshmallows with two tablespoons of water in the microwave. Microwave in thirty-second intervals, stirring after each until fully melted.

2. Grease the bowl of a stand mixer as well as the dough hook attachment with shortening.

3. Sift ¾ of the powdered sugar into the bowl and add the marshmallow mixture. Mix on low speed until it starts to come together.

4. Once it starts to pull away from the sides, generously grease your hands as well as a countertop with the shortening and knead the remaining ¼ cup of sugar into the mixture. Knead until it is smooth and pliable.

Royal Icing • • • • • • • • • • • • • • • •

Ingredients

- 2 egg whites
- 2 pounds powdered sugar
- 2 teaspoons lemon juice

1. In a standing mixer, fitted with a whisk attachment, start to whisk the egg whites and lemon juice on medium speed.

2. Slowly begin to add powdered sugar a little at a time until it is fully combined. Keep adding the sugar until it resembles a thick frosting and forms a peak when the whisk is removed. Not all of the powdered sugar will be used. To thin down the icing, add water a teaspoon at a time until the icing is fluid.

Around the World

Eskimo Cake Pops • • • • • • • • • •

Supplies

- Cake filling of your choice
- Light blue candy melts
- Peanut butter candy melts
- White candy melts
- Black candy melts
- Red petal dust

Tools

- Digital scale
- Sheet pans
- Microwave-safe bowls
- Lollipop sticks
- Plastic bags
- Soft-bristle paintbrush

1. Begin by hand weighing the cake into one-ounce portions. Roll them into balls and set aside on a sheet pan. Place in the fridge while you prepare the candy melts.

2. Melt the light blue candy melts according to the directions indicated on the package.

3. Remove the cake from the fridge. Dip the sticks into the candy melts and insert them halfway into the cake.

4. Once the candy melts have fully set and the cake is back at room temperature, the pops are ready to be dipped. Fully submerge the pops into the light blue candy melts and tap off any excess. Allow to fully set.

5. While the pops are drying, prepare the peanut butter candy melts. With the use of white or chocolate candy melts, adjust the peanut butter candy melts to achieve the desired skin tone.

6. With a spoon, scoop up the melted peanut butter candy melts and dip the front of the pops into the melts to create the face. Tap off any excess, invert, and shake from side to side to smooth out the candy melts. Allow to fully set.

7. When the faces have dried, prepare the black and white candy melts in small plastic bags and snip the corners off. With the black melts pipe on the hair, eyes, and the mouth. Allow to set.

8. The white candy melts should be slightly cool when going to pipe to create texture. Around the faces, pipe the white melts in a circular motion. Allow to set.

9. Using a small soft-bristled paintbrush, apply a small amount of red petal dust to the faces for rosy cheeks.

Hula Cake Pops

Supplies

- Cake filling of your choice
- Peanut butter candy melts
- Chocolate candy melts
- Green candy melts
- Mini daisy sprinkles

Tools

- Digital scale
- Sheet pans
- Microwave-safe bowls
- Lollipop sticks
- Plastic bags

1. Hand weigh the cake into one-ounce portions. Roll them into balls then shape into rectangles, pinching the middle in to create an hourglass figure. Make sure to flatten the top for a flat surface to work on later. Set aside on a sheet pan and place in the fridge while you prepare the candy melts.

2. Melt the peanut butter candy melts according to the directions indicated on the package. Remove the cake from the fridge. Dip the sticks into the candy melts and insert them halfway into the cake.

3. Once the candy melts have fully set and the cake is back at room temperature, the pops are ready to be dipped. Fully submerge the pops into the peanut butter candy melts and tap off any excess. Allow to fully set before moving on.

4. In plastic bags, melt the chocolate and green candy melts and snip the corners off of both. With the chocolate candy melts, pipe a horizontal line near the top and then two separate dots to create a coconut bra. Add a small dot near the bottom for the belly button.

5. When the bra and belly button have dried, pipe on strands of grass for the skirts with the green candy melts. This works best with a thick consistency. Attach the mini daisy sprinkles at the top of the skirt.

Native American Cake Pops ● ● ● ● ● ● ● ● ● ● ● ● ● ●

Supplies

- Cake filling of your choice
- Peanut butter candy melts
- Black candy melts
- Red candy melts
- Small confetti sprinkles
- Tootsie Rolls
- Fondant
- Red petal dust
- Black edible marker

Tools

- Digital scale
- Sheet pans
- Microwave-safe bowls
- Lollipop sticks
- Plastic bags
- Toothpicks
- Soft-bristle paintbrush
- Pasta machine or rolling pin
- 1$^1/_8$ inch leaf plunger

1. Prepare the feather for the Native American's headdress ahead of time. Start off by rolling out the fondant using the thickest setting on the machine, or to ⅛ of an inch thick with a rolling pin. Using a medium-sized leaf plunger, about 1⅛ inch in length, cut out the leaf shapes and allow them to dry.

2. Once the fondant has dried, dry dust the upper halves of the leaves with red petal dust. If you cannot find red petal dust, powdered food coloring will also work. Blow off any excess powder.

3. Using a black edible marker, color the tips of the leaves.

4. Prepare the cake by hand weighing it into one-ounce portions. Roll them into balls and set aside on a sheet pan. Place in the fridge while you prepare the candy melts.

5. Melt the peanut butter candy melts to create the flesh tone. Lighten or darken them with the use of white or dark chocolate if desired.

6. Remove the cake balls from the fridge. Dip the sticks into the candy melts and insert them halfway into the cake ball.

7. Dip just the tips of two small confetti sprinkles into the candy melts and attach one on each side of the cake balls for ears. Allow to set.

8. Once the candy melts have fully set and the pops are room temperature, you are ready to dip the pops. Fully submerge the pops into the candy melts and tap off any excess, keeping the faces of the pops towards you.

9. After you have dipped the pops, insert the already prepared feathers into the backs of the heads and allow the pops to set.

10. Now you need to create the headband for the pop. Knead your Tootsie Rolls until pliable. If needed, microwave it for less than ten seconds to soften it. Run it through your pasta machine and cut into quarter-inch-wide strips.

11. With a toothpick apply candy melts to the back side of the headbands and attach them to the pops just above the ears.

12. Prepare both the red and black candy melts in plastic bags, snipping off a very tiny portion of the corner to create piping bags.

13. Dip the tip of a lollipop stick into the peanut butter candy melts and dot it onto the face of the pop to create a nose. Using the red candy melts, pipe a zigzag line onto the full length of the headband. Add black dots in each triangular space on the headband. Finally, pipe on the face with the black candy melts.

Piñata Cake Pops · · · · · · · · · ·

Supplies

- Cake filling of your choice
- Pink candy melts
- Black candy melts
- Purple candy melts
- Light blue candy melts
- Yellow candy melts
- Small white confetti sprinkles
- Mini rainbow confetti sprinkles

Tools

- Sheet pans
- Microwave-safe bowls
- Lollipop sticks
- Plastic bags
- 2 x ¾ inch dog cookie cutter

1. Stuff the cookie cutter with your cake mixture, using the palm of your hand to squeeze out any excess cake. Gently push the cake out of the cookie cutter. Chilling your dough ahead of time makes this process easier.

2. Set them aside on a sheet pan and place in the fridge while you prepare the candy melts.

3. Melt the pink candy melts according to the directions indicated on the package.

4. Remove the shaped cake from the fridge. Dip the sticks into the candy melts while holding the cake with fingers both on top and underneath. Insert the sticks half way into the cake.

5. Once the candy melts have fully set and the cake is back at room temperature, you are ready to dip the pops. Fully submerge the pops into the pink candy melts and tap off any excess. Place them in your stand and allow them to fully set.

6. Once your pops are fully dried, fill a small plastic bags with the assorted colored candy melts, snip a corner off, and, starting at the base of the pop, pipe small beads of candy melts and pull back to create individual strands of melts. Allow each layer to fully dry before piping a second layer. Repeat for the full length of the pop.

7. Using the black candy melts, pipe on a harness and attach two mini confetti sprinkles at the joints of the harness. Attach a white sprinkle to the faces of the pops and add a black dot on the eyes.

Russian Doll Cake Pops ••••

Supplies

- Cake filling of your choice
- Pink candy melts
- White candy melts
- Black candy melts
- Red candy melts
- Red petal dust

Tools

- Digital scale
- Sheet pans
- Microwave-safe bowls
- Lollipop sticks
- Plastic bags
- Small stiff-bristled paintbrush

1. Hand weigh the cake into two separate portions for each pop. Roll them into balls, 0.9 of an ounce for the body and 0.4 of an ounce for the head. Set aside on a sheet pan and place in the fridge while you prepare the candy melts.

2. Melt the white candy melts according to the directions indicated on the package. Remove the cake from the fridge. Dip the sticks into the white candy melts and insert them fully through the larger cake ball, leaving ¼ inch of the sticks exposed through the top. Dip the sticks once more and attach the small balls on top.

3. Once the candy melts have fully set and the cake is back at room temperature, the pops are ready to be dipped. Fully submerge the pops into the white candy melts and tap off any excess. Allow them to set before proceeding.

4. While the pops are drying, melt the pink candy melts according to the directions indicated on the package. Once the pops are dry, dip them in the pink candy melts in a diagonal direction to create a white belly on the pops. Allow to fully set.

5. Gently tap the upper ball into a spoonful of white candy melts to create the face. Allow the excess to fall off, invert, and gently shake side to side to smooth out the face. Set aside to dry.

6. Melt the black and red candy melts in small plastic bags and snip the corners off. With the red candy melts, pipe a curved line on the white portion of the body to create the first layer of a flower. Drag the candy melts inwards with a paintbrush towards the pink part of the body. Let set and repeat to create a simple flower.

7. Using the black candy melts, pipe the hair, eyes, and mouth onto the faces. Pipe a line of black candy melts around the white of the faces and the white of the bodies. Pipe half-circles all around.

8. Lightly dust the cheeks with the red petal dust.

Baby Shower

Baby Boy Cake Pops ·······

Supplies

- Cake filling of your choice
- Peanut butter candy melts
- Light blue candy melts
- Black candy melts
- White confetti sprinkles
- Sugar pearls

Tools

- Digital scale
- Sheet pans
- Microwave-safe bowls
- Lollipop sticks
- Plastic bags
- Toothpicks

1. Begin by hand weighing the cake into one-ounce portions. Roll them into balls and set them aside on a sheet pan. Place in the fridge while you prepare the candy melts.

2. Melt the peanut butter candy melts according to the directions indicated on the package.

3. Remove the cake balls from the fridge. Dip the sticks into the candy melts and insert them halfway into the cake ball. Dip the tips of confetti sprinkles into the candy melts and attach one on each side of the ball to create the ears.

4. Once the candy melts have fully set and the cake is back at room temperature, you are ready to dip the pops. Fully submerge the pops into the candy melts and tap off any excess. Place the pops into a stand and allow them to fully dry.

5. While the pops are drying, prepare the light blue candy melts according to the directions on the package.

6. Once the pops have dried, dip a small portion of the heads just above the ears in the candy melts to create a hat. While still wet, add a sugar pearl on top and place in the stand to set.

7. Put some of the melted light blue candy melts into a plastic bag and snip off a small corner. You want to use melts that have cooled enough to be slightly thick and maintain a shape. Pipe a boarder of melts around the entire rim of the hat.

8. Create another piping bag filled with peanut butter candy melts, pipe on dots for the noses, and let them fully set.

9. Once the nose has set, glue on white confetti sprinkles for eyes with a toothpick and candy melts. Dot the eyes with black candy melts for the pupils.

10. Using the same light blue candy melts used for the rim of the hat, pipe small circles on the face for the bases of the pacifiers. Allow to set, then pipe smaller rings around the bases and add dots to the top of the pacifier.

Baby Girl Cake Pops • • • • • • •

Supplies

- Cake filling of your choice
- Peanut butter candy melts
- Pink candy melts
- Black candy melts
- White confetti sprinkles
- Red petal dust

Tools

- Digital scale
- Sheet pans
- Microwave-safe bowls
- Lollipop sticks
- Plastic bags
- Toothpicks
- Soft-bristle paintbrush

1. Begin by hand weighing the cake into one-ounce portions. Roll them into balls and set them aside on a sheet pan. Place in the fridge while you prepare the candy melts.

2. Melt the peanut butter candy melts according to the directions indicated on the package.

3. Remove the cake balls from the fridge. Dip the sticks into the candy melts and insert them halfway into the cake ball. Dip the tips of confetti sprinkles into the candy melts and attach one on each side of the balls to create the ears.

4. Once the candy melts have fully set and the cake is back at room temperature, you are ready to dip the pops. Fully submerge the pops into the candy melts and tap off any excess. Place the pops into a stand and allow them to fully dry.

5. Create a piping bag filled with peanut butter candy melts, pipe on dots for the noses, and let it fully set.

6. Glue on white confetti sprinkles for eyes with a toothpick and candy melts.

7. Prepare the black and pink candy melts in plastic bags and snip off a small corner of each bag. Using the black, dot the eyes and pipe in a strand of hair near the tops of the heads.

8. Using the pink candy melts, pipe on a bow and a small circle on the faces for the bases of the pacifiers. Allow to set, then pipe a smaller ring around the base and add dots to the tops of the pacifiers. Allow to fully set.

9. When the pacifier has set, dry brush the cheeks with red petal dust.

Baby Monkey Cake Pops • • • •

Supplies

- Cake filling of your choice
- Chocolate candy melts
- Peanut butter candy melts
- Light blue candy melts
- Smarties

Tools

- Digital scale
- Sheet pans
- Microwave-safe bowls
- Lollipop sticks
- Plastic bags

1. Begin by hand weighing the cake into one-ounce portions. Roll them into balls and set aside on a sheet pan. Place in the fridge while you prepare the candy melts.

2. Melt the chocolate candy melts according to the directions indicated on the package.

3. Remove the cake balls from the fridge. Dip the sticks into the candy melts and insert them halfway into the cake balls. Attach a Smartie on each side of the balls using candy melts.

4. Once the candy melts have fully set and the cake is back at room temperature, you are ready to dip the pops. Fully submerge the pops into the candy melts and tap off any excess. Place in a stand and allow to set.

5. Prepare the peanut butter melts in a small plastic bag and snip off a corner to create a piping bag. Make sure your chocolate is warm and fluid for best results.

6. On the front of the pops, pipe the outline of the faces smaller than what you want the actual face to be. Flood the outline with the candy melts and then gently tap the pop face-side up to smooth out the face. Then pipe a dot of melted peanut butter melts on each ear and allow to set.

7. When the face has set, pipe on the eyes and nose with the chocolate candy melts.

8. Using light blue candy melts, pipe a small circle on the face for the base of the pacifier. Allow to set, then pipe a smaller ring around the base created and add dot to the top of the pacifier. Allow to fully set.

Note

To keep the pops in place while you pipe on the face, fill a plastic bag with rice and use it as a cushion to keep the pop still.

Variation

You can create a variety of monkeys for different events by playing around with the basic cake pop shape. Try adding a pink bow for a girl monkey, a gold crown for a king of the jungle party, or a fondant party hat for quick birthday pops.

Button Cake Pops

Supplies

- Cake filling of your choice
- Pink candy melts
- Black candy melts

Tools

- Digital scale
- Sheet pans
- Microwave-safe bowls
- Lollipop sticks
- Plastic bags
- 1¼ inch circle cookie cutter with rounded edge

1. Begin by hand weighing the cake into one-ounce portions. Roll them into balls and flatten the tops so each ball is at least 1½ inches in diameter.

2. Use a cookie cutter with a rounded edge that is approximately 1¼ inches in diameter and create an indentation on top of the flattened cake balls to create the rim of the button. With the end of a lollipop stick, create four indentations for the buttonholes. Set aside on a sheet pan and place in the fridge while you prepare the candy melts.

3. Melt the pink candy melts according to the directions indicated on the package.

4. Remove the cake from the fridge. Dip the sticks into the candy melts and insert them halfway into the cake.

5. Once the candy melts have fully set and the cake is back at room temperature, you are ready to dip the pops. Fully submerge the pops into the candy melts and tap off any excess. When tapping off the excess, have the back of the pops facing you. Place the pops in a stand and allow them to fully dry.

6. While the pops are drying, put the black candy melts in a plastic bag and snip off a small corner. Fill the four indentations with the black melts and connect opposite holes to creating the visual effect of thread.

Note

For this recipe you want to use a cake that is really moist and pliable so that the cake edges do not split and crack when flattened.

Teddy Bear Cake Pops ......

Supplies

- Cake filling of your choice
- Chocolate candy melts
- Peanut butter candy melts
- Black candy melts

Tools

- Sheet pans
- Microwave-safe bowls
- Lollipop sticks
- Plastic bags
- 1½ x ¾ inch teddy bear cookie cutter

1. Stuff the cookie cutter with the cake mixture, using the palm of your hand to squeeze out any excess cake. Gently push the cake out of the cookie cutter. Chilling your dough ahead of time makes this process easier.

2. Set them aside on a sheet pan and place in the fridge while you prepare the candy melts.

3. Melt the chocolate, peanut butter, and black candy melts according to the directions indicated on the package. Put the peanut butter and black candy melts in plastic bags, snip off the corners of the bags, and set aside.

4. Remove the shaped cake from the fridge. Dip the sticks into the candy melts while holding the cake with fingers, both on top and underneath, and insert sticks halfway into the cake.

5. Once the candy melts have fully set and the cake is back at room temperature, you are ready to dip the pops. Fully submerge the pops into the chocolate candy melts and tap off any excess. Allow to set in stand.

6. When the pops are fully dried, pipe on the bellies, snouts, and dots for ears and paws with the peanut butter candy melts.

7. Using the black candy melts, pipe on the eyes and noses of the bears.

Dinosaurs

Dino Egg Cake Pops ·······

Supplies

- Cake filling of your choice
- White candy melts
- Yellow petal dust
- Orange petal dust
- Brown petal dust
- Green luster dust

Tools

- Digital scale
- Sheet pans
- Microwave-safe bowls
- Lollipop sticks
- Soft-bristle paintbrush

1. Begin by hand weighing the cake into one-ounce portions. Roll them into an egg shape and set them aside on a sheet pan. Place in the fridge while you prepare the candy melts.

2. Melt the white candy melts according to the directions indicated on the package.

3. Remove the cake from the fridge. Dip the sticks into the candy melts and insert them halfway into the cake.

4. Once the candy melts have fully set and the cake is back at room temperature, you are ready to dip the pops. Fully submerge the pops into the candy melts and tap off any excess. Place the pops into a stand and allow them to fully dry.

5. Once the pops have fully dried, dry dust the pops with the paintbrush, starting with the yellow petal dust. Repeat the same steps for the orange and brown petal dust, blending the various colors.

6. Finish it off with the green luster dust to add sparkle.

Note

If you want an egg with more of a textured finish, roll a piece of aluminum foil into a small ball and roll it around the cake to texturize the egg before dipping.

Dinosaur Cake Pops · · · · · · ·

Supplies

- Cake filling of your choice
- Purple candy melts
- Black candy melts
- Red jumbo heart sprinkles
- Green mini confetti sprinkles
- Tic Tacs

Tools

- Digital scale
- Sheet pans
- Microwave-safe bowls
- Lollipop sticks
- Plastic bag

1. Begin by hand weighing the cake into one-ounce portions. Roll them into balls. Place a finger on opposite sides of the balls and roll to slightly elongate ends to create the head and tail. Place in the fridge while you prepare the candy melts.

2. Melt the purple candy melts according to the directions indicated on the package.

3. Remove the cake from the fridge. Dip the sticks into the candy melts and insert them halfway into the cake. Dip the tips of four Tic Tacs into the candy melts and insert them into the bottoms of the cake for the feet.

4. Once the candy melts have fully set and the cake is back at room temperature, the pops are ready to be dipped. Fully submerge the pops into the purple candy melts and tap off any excess.

5. While still wet, attach five heart sprinkles along the spines of the pops pointed-side up and allow to set. Once set, attach a random amount of the green confetti sprinkles to the sides of the bodies.

6. In a small plastic bag, prepare the black candy melts and pipe on the eyes.

Fossil Cake Pops ● ● ● ● ● ● ● ● ● ●

Supplies

- Cake filling of your choice
- Peanut butter candy melts
- White candy melts
- Black candy color
- Brown petal dust

Tools

- Digital scale
- Sheet pans
- Microwave-safe bowls
- Lollipop sticks
- Plastic bags
- Chocolate leaf mold
- Soft-bristle paintbrush

1. Begin by hand weighing the cake into one-ounce portions. Roughly roll them into small nugget shapes on a flat surface. The more rock-like you make them look the better; they do not need to be perfect. Set them aside on a sheet pan and place in the fridge while you prepare the candy melts.

2. Melt the white candy melts according to the directions indicated on the package and add a few drops of black candy color to create a light gray. Fill a plastic bag with the gray candy melts to create a piping bag. Pipe the candy melts into the leaf molds and allow to fully set. Once set, remove them from the molds and set aside.

3. Melt the peanut butter candy melts according to the directions indicated on the package. Remove the shaped cake from the fridge. Dip the sticks into the candy melts and insert them halfway into the cake.

4. Once the candy melts have fully set and the cake is back at room temperature, you are ready to dip the pops. Fully submerge the pops into the candy melts and tap off any excess.

5. While the pops are still wet, place a leaf that was created earlier in the center of the pops, using the candy melts, and allow to set in a stand.

6. Once dried, dust the petal dust, using a paintbrush, onto the pop, focusing mainly on the leaves. Dust them until they are brown and just the gray vein is showing through. Then lightly dry dust the full pop and highlight the edges.

Volcano Cake Pops

Supplies

- Cake filling of your choice
- Chocolate candy melts
- Red candy melts
- Orange candy melts
- Yellow candy melts

Tools

- Digital scale
- Sheet pans
- Microwave-safe bowls
- Lollipop sticks
- Plastic bags
- Small pallet knife

1. Begin by hand weighing the cake into one-ounce portions. Roll them into a rough volcanic cone shape. Once you have the basic shape, make sure to flatten the edges on the counter with your fingertips and create various indentations. Set them aside on a sheet pan and place in the fridge while you prepare the candy melts.

2. Melt the chocolate candy melts according to the directions indicated on the package.

3. Remove the shaped cake from the fridge. Dip the sticks into the candy melts and insert them halfway into the cake.

4. Once the candy melts have fully set and the cake is back at room temperature, you are ready to dip the pops. Fully submerge the pops into the candy melts and tap off any excess.

5. While the pops are still wet, drag the blunt side of a knife up and down the pop to create ridges. Allow it to fully set and repeat the process with the chocolate candy melts. As the candy melts cool, a rocky texture will be created.

6. Melt the red, yellow, and orange candy melts, then mix them together in a plastic bag by slightly squeezing it. Cut off a corner and pipe the lava onto the pops.

Enchanted

Fairy Wand Cake Pops ● ● ● ● ● ●

Supplies

- Cake filling of your choice
- White candy melts
- Green candy melts
- Disco dust
- Purple fondant

Tools

- Sheet pans
- Microwave-safe bowls
- Lollipop sticks
- Paintbrush
- 2 x ¾ inch star cookie cutter
- Pasta machine
- Mini flower plunger

1. Stuff the cookie cutter with the cake mixture, using the palm of your hand to squeeze out any excess cake. Gently push the cake out of the cookie cutter. Soften the edges of the star by pushing down all sharp edges with your fingertips. Chilling your dough ahead of time makes this process easier.

2. Set them aside on a sheet pan and place in the fridge while you prepare the candy melts.

3. Melt the white candy melts according to the directions indicated on the package.

4. Remove the cake from the fridge. Dip the sticks into the candy melts while holding the cake with fingers, both on top and underneath, and insert sticks halfway into the cake.

5. Once the candy melts have fully set and the cake is back at room temperature, you are ready to dip the pops. Fully submerge the pops into the candy melts and tap off any excess.

6. With a dry paintbrush pick up some disco dust and tap it onto the pops while the candy melts are still wet. Place in a stand and allow to set.

7. While the pops are drying, prepare the flowers for the wands by rolling out the purple fondant on the thickest setting on a pasta machine and useing a flower plunger to cut out mini flowers.

8. Prepare the green melts in a small plastic bag and snip off a corner to create a piping bag. Make sure the candy melts are warm and fluid for best results. Pipe on a letter of your choosing in cursive and attach the purple flower to it.

Frog Prince Cake Pops • • • • •

Supplies

- Cake filling of your choice
- Green candy melts
- Black candy melts
- White Sixlets
- Fondant
- Edible gold spray

Tools

- Digital scale
- Sheet pans
- Microwave-safe bowls
- Lollipop sticks
- Plastic bag
- Pasta machine
- Wooden spoon

1. Roll out fondant ahead of time using the thickest setting on a pasta machine and cut out half-inch-wide strips. Cut out triangles from the strips to create the points of the crown. Wrap the fondant completely around the handle of a wooden spoon and smooth out the seams. Slightly curl the points of the triangles and gently slide them off the spoon. Allow them to fully harden. Spray them with edible gold spray and set them aside.

2. Hand weigh the cake into one-ounce portions. Roll them into balls and set aside on a sheet pan. Place in the fridge while you prepare the candy melts.

3. Melt the green candy melts according to the directions indicated on the package.

4. Remove the cake from the fridge. Dip the sticks into the candy melts and insert them halfway into the cake.

5. Once the candy melts have fully set and the cake is back at room temperature, the pops are ready to be dipped. Fully submerge the pops into the green candy melts and tap off any excess.

6. While the top is still wet, place two Sixlets for the eyes and place the crown behind them. Allow to fully set.

7. Place melted black candy melts in a small plastic bag, snip the corner off, and pipe on the mouth, nostrils, and eyes.

Sugar Fairy Cake Pops ● ● ● ● ●

Supplies

- Cake filling of your choice
- Red candy melts
- White candy melts
- Red sanding sugar
- Fondant

Tools

- Digital scale
- Sheet pans
- Microwave-safe bowls
- Lollipop sticks
- Plastic bag
- Pasta machine
- $1^1/_8$ inch butterfly cutter

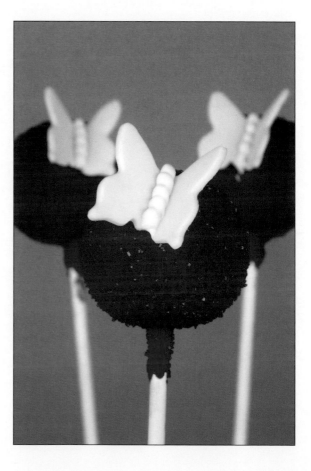

1. Roll out fondant ahead of time with the thickest setting on a pasta machine and use a small butterfly cutter to cut out butterflies. With either a small box or the edge of your counter, place the butterflies on a corner and fold the wings over so that they maintain a v shape. Allow to fully dry before using.

2. Begin by hand weighing the cake into one-ounce portions. Roll them into balls and set aside on a sheet pan. Place in the fridge while you prepare the candy melts.

3. Melt the red candy melts according to the directions indicated on the package.

4. Remove the cake from the fridge. Dip the sticks into the candy melts and insert them halfway into the cake.

5. Once the candy melts have fully set and the cake is back at room temperature, the pops are ready to be dipped. Fully submerge the pops into the red candy melts and tap off any excess.

6. While still wet, cover the entire pop with sanding sugar. Once they are fully covered, place a butterfly on each pop before the candy melts set.

7. Once the melts have set, melt the white candy melts in a small plastic bag, snip off the corner, and pipe the body in the center of the wings

Note

Made sure to tap off all the excess candy melts before covering with sugar, as the weight from the sugar will pull the melts off and cause the sugar coating to fall off. Make sure the candy coating is fluid before dipping to avoid this.

Tower Cake Pops

Supplies

- Cake filling of your choice
- White candy melts
- Black candy melts
- Green candy melts
- Hershey's Kisses
- Purple fondant

Tools

- Digital scale
- Sheet pans
- Microwave-safe bowls
- Lollipop sticks
- Plastic bags
- Pasta machine
- ¾ inch small rose petal cutter

1. Begin by hand weighing the cake into one-ounce portions. Roll each into a log that is as thick as a Hershey's Kiss. Set them aside on a sheet pan and place in the fridge while you prepare the candy melts.

2. Melt the white candy melts according to the directions indicated on the package.

3. Remove the cake from the fridge. Dip the sticks into the melted candy melts and insert them halfway into the cake.

4. Once the candy melts have fully set and the cake is back at room temperature, you are ready to dip the pops. Fully submerge the pops into the white candy melts and tap off any excess.

5. While still wet, attach a Hershey's Kiss to the top of the pop and allow to set in a stand.

6. In a small plastic bag, melt the black and green candy melts separately, snip off a corner in each, and set aside. When the pops have dried, pipe on a window with the black candy melts and allow to set.

7. Once it has set, fill a plastic bag with melted white candy melts and pipe on dots around the window, leaving space. Allow those dots to set, and in the empty spaces pipe additional dots. Around the pop, pipe on additional bricks with the white melts.

8. Taking the green melts, pipe on vines, going the full length of the towers. Once the vines have set, pipe on the leaves by piping dots and pulling up. A thick chocolate works best.

9. Roll the purple fondant out on the thickest setting on the pasta machine and cut out shingles using a small rose petal cutter. Glue the fondant shingles onto the Hershey's Kisses with candy melts until they are fully covered.

Unicorn Cake Pops •••••••••

Supplies

- Cake filling of your choice
- White candy melts
- Pink candy melts
- Purple candy melts
- Black candy melts
- Jumbo heart sprinkles
- Gold luster dust
- Fondant

Tools

- Digital scale
- Sheet pans
- Microwave-safe bowls
- Lollipop sticks
- Toothpicks
- Plastic bags

1. Begin by hand weighing the cake into one-ounce portions. Roll them into balls and then sculpt pear shapes, so that the nose end is narrower than the head. Set aside on a sheet pan and place in the fridge while you prepare the candy melts.

2. Melt the white candy melts according to the directions indicated on the package.

3. Remove the cake from the fridge. Dip the sticks into the candy melts and insert them halfway into the cake. Dip the rounded ends of the heart sprinkles into the candy melts and insert them on opposite ends of the heads to create ears.

4. Once the candy melts have fully set and the cake is back at room temperature, the pops are ready to be dipped. Fully submerge the pops into the white candy melts and tap off any excess. Allow to set in a stand.

5. While the pops are drying, roll small balls of fondant into cones and carve spirals with a toothpick for horns. Pour some of the gold luster dust in a small bag and place the fondant cones inside. Shake the bag until all the cones are gold.

6. Place melted pink and purple candy melts in a single plastic bag together and snip off a corner. You want the melts to be slightly thick so that they hold their shape when piped. Attach the fondant cones between the ears using candy melts. Around the cones, pipe individual strands of hair for the mane and allow to set.

7. While the pops are drying, place melted black candy melts in a plastic bag and snip off a corner. Pipe on the eyes as well as the nostrils.

Wizard Hat Cake Pops • • • • •

Supplies

- Cake filling of your choice
- Blue candy melts
- Disco dust
- Silver edible luster spray
- Fondant

Tools

- Digital scale
- Sheet pans
- Microwave-safe bowls
- Lollipop sticks
- Toothpicks
- ½ inch star fondant cutter
- Pasta machine
- Paintbrush

1. Begin by hand weighing the cake into one-ounce portions. Roll them into cones and set aside on a sheet pan. Place in the fridge while you prepare the candy melts.

2. Melt the blue candy melts according to the directions indicated on the package.

3. Remove the cake from the fridge. Dip the sticks into the candy melts and insert them halfway into the cake.

4. Once the candy melts have fully set and the cake is back at room temperature, you are ready to dip the pops. Fully submerge the pops into the candy melts and tap off any excess.

5. Tap some disco dust onto the pops with a dry paintbrush while the candy melts are still wet. Place in a stand and allow to set.

6. While the pops are drying, prepare the stars for the hat by rolling out fondant on the thickest setting on a pasta machine and cutting out stars using the mini star cutter. Spray the stars with edible luster spray.

7. When the pops and luster spray have dried, attach them to the hats with candy melts and a toothpick.

Note

If you cannot find edible luster spray you can also dry dust the stars with silver luster dust.

On the Farm

Chicken Cake Pops••••••••

Supplies

- Cake filling of your choice
- White candy melts
- Black candy melts
- Red candy melts
- Red sprinkle sparks
- Orange rainbow chips

Tools

- Digital scale
- Sheet pans
- Microwave-safe bowls
- Lollipop sticks
- Plastic bags
- Stiff-bristle paintbrush

1. Begin by hand weighing the cake into one-ounce portions. Roll them into balls and set aside on a sheet pan. Place in the fridge while you prepare the candy melts.

2. Melt the white candy melts according to the directions indicated on the package.

3. Remove the cake from the fridge. Dip the sticks into the candy melts and insert them halfway into the cake.

4. Once the candy melts have fully set and the cake is back at room temperature, the pops are ready to be dipped. Fully submerge the pops into the white candy melts and tap off any excess.

5. While still wet, attach five red sprinkle sparks to the tops of the pops and allow to fully set.

6. In small plastic bag, prepare the red and black melts and snip off a corner. On the front of the pop, pipe two dots for the eyes with the black melts. Pipe on the chicken's wattle with the red melts and place the orange rainbow chip for the beak. Allow to fully set.

7. Paint on the wings with the white candy melts.

Cow Cake Pops ● ● ● ● ● ● ● ● ● ● ●

Supplies

- Cake filling of your choice
- White candy melts
- Pink candy melts
- Black candy melts
- Fondant

Tools

- Pasta machine
- Digital scale
- Sheet pans
- Microwave-safe bowls
- Lollipop sticks
- Toothpicks
- Plastic bags
- ¾ inch small rose petal cutter

1. Roll out the fondant ahead of time on the thickest setting on the pasta machine and cut out two petals for each pop with the small rose petal cutter. Pinch the rounded ends together and allow to fully harden.

2. Hand weigh the cake into one-ounce portions. Roll them into balls and sculpt into pear shapes. Set aside on a sheet pan and place in the fridge while you prepare the candy melts.

3. Melt the white candy melts according to the directions indicated on the package.

4. Remove the cake from the fridge. Dip the sticks into the candy melts and insert them halfway into the cake at a slight angle in the back of the narrow end. Dip the pinched section of the ears created earlier into the candy melts and attach to the tops of the heads.

5. Once the candy melts have fully set and the cake is back at room temperature, the pops are ready to be dipped. Fully submerge the pops into the white candy melts and tap off any excess. Allow to set in a stand.

6. While the pops are drying, melt the pink candy melts according to the directions indicated on the package. Once dried, slightly dip the bottom portion of the pop to create the mouth areas and allow to set.

7. While the pops are drying, place the melted black and pink candy melts in plastic bags and snip off a corner. Using the black melts, pipe on spots, the eyes, the nostrils, and the mouth. With the pink melts pipe the inner ears and allow to set.

Horse Cake Pops

Ingredients

- Cake filling of your choice
- Chocolate candy melts
- Peanut butter candy melts
- Red candy melts
- Black candy melts
- Jumbo heart sprinkles

Tools

- Digital scale
- Sheet pans
- Microwave-safe bowls
- Lollipop sticks
- Plastic bags

1. Begin by hand weighing the cake into one-ounce portions, then roll each one into a ball. Place a finger on the edge of each ball and roll to create a pear shape. Shape it so that the nose end is narrower than the head of the horse. Set these aside on a sheet pan and place in the fridge while you prepare the candy melts.

2. Melt the chocolate candy melts according to the directions indicated on the package.

3. Remove the cake balls from the fridge. Dip the tops of the lollipop sticks into the melted chocolate and then insert them halfway into the cake.

4. Dip the rounded ends of each jumbo heart sprinkle into the chocolate candy melts (so the triangle part sticks out) and insert them on opposite sides of the heads to create ears.

5. Once the candy melts have fully set and the cake is back at room temperature, the pops are ready to be dipped. Fully submerge the pops in the remaining melted chocolate and tap off any excess. Allow to set in a stand.

6. Place the melted red, black, and peanut butter candy melts in plastic bags and snip off corners. With the red melts, pipe a circle around the mouth and a line going from the center of the circles to the back of the ears. Using the black melts, pipe on the eyes as well as the nostrils. Allow to set.

7. Once the icing has set, pipe on the hair using the peanut butter melts. You want the peanut butter melts to be slightly thick. Starting behind the ears, pipe a dot and drag it forward to create a strand of hair. Repeat until you have a full mane.

Pig Cake Pops • • • • • • • • • • •

Supplies

- Cake filling of your choice
- Pink candy melts
- Black candy melts
- Jumbo heart sprinkles
- Smarties

Tools

- Digital scale
- Sheet pans
- Microwave-safe bowls
- Lollipop sticks
- Plastic bag

1. Begin by hand weighing the cake into one-ounce portions. Roll them into balls and set aside on a sheet pan. Place in the fridge while you prepare the candy melts.

2. Melt the pink candy melts according to the directions indicated on the package.

3. Remove the cake from the fridge. Dip the sticks into the candy melts and insert them halfway into the cake. Next dip the rounded ends of the heart sprinkles into the candy melts and attach them to the top of the cake to create ears.

Add a dot of the candy melts to the front and attach a Smartie for the snout.

4. Once the candy melts have fully set and the cake is back at room temperature, the pops are ready to be dipped. Fully submerge the pops into the pink candy melts and tap off any excess. Allow the candy melts to fully set.

5. In a small plastic bag prepare the black melts and snip off a corner. On the front of the pops, pipe two dots for the eyes as well as two smaller dots on top of the snouts for nostrils.

Fun Designs

Alien Cake Pops • • • • • • • • • • •

Supplies

- Cake filling of your choice
- Purple candy melts
- Green candy-coated sunflower seeds

Tools

- Digital scale
- Sheet pans
- Microwave-safe bowls
- Lollipop sticks
- Plastic bag

1. Begin by hand weighing the cake into one-ounce portions. Roll them into pear shapes and set aside on a sheet pan. Place in the fridge while you prepare the candy melts.

2. Melt the purple candy melts according to the directions indicated on the package.

3. Remove the cake from the fridge. Dip the sticks into the candy melts and insert them into the narrow end of the cake. Dip the rounded ends of the candy-coated sunflower seeds in the candy melts and attach them to the sides of the pops.

4. Once the candy melts have fully set and the cake is back at room temperature, the pops are ready to be dipped. Fully submerge the pops into the purple candy melts and tap off any excess.

5. While still wet, attach the green candy-coated sunflower seeds to the faces of the pops to create the eyes. Allow the candy melts to fully set.

6. In a small plastic bags, pour some of the prepared purple melts and snip off a corner. Pipe veins all over the head.

Ammo Cake Pops • • • • • • • • • •

Supplies

- Cake filling of your choice
- Peanut butter candy melts
- Black candy melts
- Brown petal dust
- Black petal dust
- Black sanding sugar

Tools

- Digital scale
- Sheet pans
- Microwave-safe bowls
- Lollipop sticks
- Toothpicks
- Plastic bag

1. Begin by hand weighing the cake into one-ounce portions and shape them into rectangles. Round out the bottom corners and with a toothpick create various indentations to make them resemble sacks. Set aside on a sheet pan and place in the fridge while you prepare the candy melts.

2. Melt the peanut butter candy melts according to the directions indicated on the package.

3. Remove the cake from the fridge. Dip the sticks into the candy melts and insert them halfway into the cake. Once the candy melts have fully set and the cake is back at room temperature, the pops are ready to be dipped. Fully submerge the pops into the candy melts and tap off any excess. Allow to set in a stand.

4. Once the pops have dried, lightly dry dust them with the brown and black petal dust.

5. Melt the black candy melts in a plastic bag and snip off a corner. Pipe three Xs on the fronts of the pops and a small puddle of candy melts on the tops of the pops. While the small puddle is still wet, apply black sanding sugar.

Artist Palette Cake Pops • • •

Supplies

- Cake filling of your choice
- Chocolate candy melts
- Red candy melts
- Orange candy melts
- Yellow candy melts
- Green candy melts
- Blue candy melts

Tools

- Digital scale
- Sheet pans
- Microwave-safe bowls
- Lollipop sticks
- Plastic bags
- Small paintbrush
- Toothpicks

1. Begin by hand weighing the cake into one-ounce portions. Shape the cake into paint palettes. Flatten the tops of them slightly with the back of an object that has a flat surface or the palm of your hand. Using the end of a small paintbrush that is at least a quarter-inch wide, create an indentation on the upper-right corner of the palette.

2. Set them aside on a sheet pan and place in the fridge while you prepare the candy melts.

3. Melt the chocolate candy melts according to the directions indicated on the package.

4. Remove the shaped cake from the fridge. Dip the sticks into the candy melts and, while holding the cake with fingers both on top and underneath, insert sticks halfway into the cake.

5. Once the candy melts have fully set and the cake is back at room temperature, you are ready to dip the pops. Fully submerge the pops into the candy melts and tap off any excess. Place the pops into a stand and allow them to fully dry.

6. While the pops are drying, place the melted red, orange, yellow, green, and blue candy melts in small plastic bags and snip off the tips of the bags.

7. When the pops are dried, pipe small dots of the various colored candy melts onto them. Take a toothpick and smear the edges to make it look like splatters of paint.

Colorful Bear Cake Pops • • •

Supplies

- Cake filling of your choice
- Candy melts of your choice
- Sanding sugar of your choice
- Small white confetti sprinkles
- Black candy melts
- Fondant

Tools

- Sheet Pans
- Microwave-safe bowls
- Lollipop sticks
- Plastic bags
- Toothpicks
- 1½ x ¾ inch teddy bear cookie cutter
- ½ inch heart fondant cutter
- Pasta machine

1. Stuff the cookie cutter with the cake mixture, using the palm of your hand to squeeze out any excess cake. Gently push the cake out of the cookie cutter. Chilling your dough ahead of time makes this process easier.

2. Set them aside on a sheet pan and place in the fridge while you prepare the candy melts.

3. Melt the colored candy melts according to the directions indicated on the package.

4. Remove the shaped cake from the fridge. Dip the sticks into the candy melts while holding the cake with fingers, both on top and underneath and insert sticks halfway into the cake.

5. Once the candy melts have fully set and the cake is back at room temperature, you are ready to dip the pops. Fully submerge the pops into the candy melts and tap off any excess.

6. While the pops are still wet, pour the sanding sugar of your choice over the pop to cover any exposed chocolate. Use the same colored sugar as the color candy melts.

7. Place them in a stand and allow them to fully set.

8. While the pops are drying, roll out the fondant on the thickest setting of the pasta machine and cut out the heart shapes.

9. Once the pops are fully dried, with a toothpick and candy melts glue both the white confetti sprinkle on as a nose and the heart onto the belly of the bear.

10. Next, prepare the black candy melts in a small plastic bag and cut off the tip of the bag. Pipe on both the eyes and nose of the bear.

Monster Cake Pops • • • • • • •

Supplies

- Cake filling of your choice
- Red candy melts
- Black candy melts
- White Sixlets

Tools

- Digital scale
- Sheet pans
- Microwave-safe bowls
- Lollipop sticks
- Plastic bags

1. Begin by hand weighing the cake into one-ounce portions. Roll them into balls and set aside on a sheet pan. Place in the fridge while you prepare the chocolate.

2. Melt the red candy melts according to the directions indicated on the package.

3. Remove the cake from the fridge. Dip the sticks into the candy melts and insert them halfway into the cake.

4. Once the candy melts have fully set and the cake is back at room temperature, the pops are ready to be dipped. Fully submerge the pops into the red candy melts and tap off any excess. Allow to set in a stand.

5. Fill a plastic bag with the red candy melts and snip off a small corner. Drizzle the melts all over the pops and allow to set. Once set, pipe on another layer of drizzles to cover any smooth spaces. It works best if the candy melts are thick. While still wet, attach three Sixlets to the front of the pops. Allow to set.

6. Once the candy melts have set, prepare the black candy melts in a small plastic bag, snip the corner off, and pipe dots on to all the Sixlets.

Mustache Cake Pops • • • • • •

Supplies

- Cake filling of your choice
- White candy melts
- Black candy melts

Tools

- Digital scale
- Sheet pans
- Microwave-safe bowls
- Lollipop sticks
- Plastic bags

1. Begin by hand weighing the cake into one-ounce portions. Roll them into balls and set aside on a sheet pan. Place in the fridge while you prepare the candy melts.

2. Melt the white candy melts according to the directions indicated on the package.

3. Remove the cake balls from the fridge. Dip the sticks into the candy melts and insert them halfway into the cake balls.

4. Once the candy melts have fully set and the cake is back at room temperature, you are ready to dip the pops. Fully submerge the pops into the candy melts and tap off any excess. Place the pops into a stand and allow them to fully dry.

5. While the pops are drying, melt the black candy melts in a small plastic bag and cut off the tip of the bag.

6. Once the pops are dried, pipe the outline of a mustache onto each and fill them in. Allow the candy melts to fully set.

7. Once the mustache sets and hardens, pipe on fine lines to create the individual strands of hair, leaving space between each strand.

8. Allow the first layer of piped hair to fully set, then go back and add another layer until you have created a bushy mustache.

Nail Polish Cake Pops • • • • • • •

Supplies

- Cake filling of your choice
- Red candy melts
- Black candy melts
- Tootsie Rolls
- Disco dust

Tools

- Digital scale
- Sheet pans
- Microwave-safe bowls
- Lollipop sticks
- Stiff-bristle paintbrush

1. Begin by hand weighing the cake into one-ounce portions. Roll them into balls and set aside on a sheet pan. Place in the fridge while you prepare the candy melts.

2. Melt the red candy melts according to the directions indicated on the package.

3. Remove the cake from the fridge. Dip the sticks into the candy melts and insert them halfway into the cake. Attach a Tootsie Roll to the top of the pop with candy melts.

4. Once the candy melts have fully set and the cake is back at room temperature, the pops are ready to be dipped. Fully submerge the pops into the red candy melts and tap off any excess.

5. While the pops are still wet, dip a stiff-bristle paintbrush into the disco dust and tap it over the wet candy melts. Focus mainly around the cake portion, as the Tootsie Roll portion will be covered up. Set aside and allow to set.

6. While the candy melts are drying, prepare the black candy melts. Once the pops have dried, dip the Tootsie Roll portion of the pops into the black melts and tap off the excess. Allow to fully set.

Peace Cake Pops · · · · · · · · ·

Supplies

- Cake filling of your choice
- White candy melts
- Pink candy melts
- Yellow candy melts
- Orange candy melts
- Purple candy melts
- Purple sanding sugar

Tools

- Digital scale
- Sheet pans
- Microwave-safe bowls
- Lollipop sticks
- Plastic bags

1. Begin by hand weighing the cake into one-ounce portions. Roll them into balls and slightly flatten them. Set them aside on a sheet pan and place in the fridge while you prepare the candy melts.

2. Melt the white candy melts according to the directions indicated on the package.

3. Remove the cake from the fridge. Dip the sticks into the melted white candy melts and insert them halfway into the cake.

4. Prepare the yellow, orange, and pink candy melts in small plastic bags, snip the corners off, and set aside.

5. Once the candy melts have fully set and the cake is back at room temperature, you are ready to dip the pops. Fully submerge the pops into the white candy melts and tap off any excess.

6. While still wet, drizzle the pink, orange, and yellow candy melts on the pop and tap over a separate bowl to remove the excess. Set aside and allow to set.

7. Prepare the purple melts in a small plastic bag and snip the corner off. On the pops draw on a peace symbol, then sprinkle the purple sanding sugar over the candy melts.

Piggy Bank Cake Pops ● ● ● ● ● ●

Supplies

- Cake filling of your choice
- Purple candy melts
- Black candy melts
- Jumbo heart sprinkles
- Yellow jumbo confetti sprinkles
- Mini black confetti sprinkles
- Smarties
- Tic Tacs
- Edible gold luster spray

Tools

- Digital scale
- Sheet pans
- Microwave-safe bowls
- Lollipop sticks
- Toothpick

1. Begin by hand weighing the cake into one-ounce portions. Roll them into slightly elongated balls and set aside on a sheet pan. Place in a fridge while you prepare the candy melts.

2. Melt the purple candy melts according to the directions indicated on the package.

3. Remove the cake from the fridge. Dip the sticks into the candy melts and insert them halfway into the cake ball. Next dip the round ends of the heart sprinkles into the melts and attach them to the tops of the cake balls. Next dip four Tic-Tacs in the melts and attach them to the bottom of the ball for the feet. With a toothpick you will need to apply a drop of the melts where you want the nose to be and attach a Smartie.

4. While the candy melts dry, prepare the gold coins. Spray the yellow confetti sprinkles with edible gold luster spray. Set aside and allow to dry.

5. Once the candy melts have fully set and the cake is back at room temperature, you are ready to dip the pops. Fully submerge the pops into the candy melts and tap off any excess. Keep the face of the pig towards you as you tap off the excess.

6. While still wet, insert the gold coins halfway into the tops of the pigs and allow the pops to fully set in a stand.

7. Prepare the black candy melts in a plastic bag and snip off a corner. Once your pop is fully dry pipe a dollar sign on the side of it.

8. Dip a toothpick into the melted purple candy melts and dot on where the eyes will go. Attach the black confetti sprinkles and allow to set.

Note

If you cannot find edible luster spray you can paint the coins gold with gold luster dust and flavorless vodka or lemon juice. Put a small amount of luster dust in a small container, add a drop of vodka or lemon juice, and stir with a paintbrush until the two have combined and formed a paint-like consistency. Paint it on and allow to fully dry before handling.

Robot Cake Pops

Supplies

- Cake filling of your choice
- White candy melts
- Black candy color
- Black candy melts
- Green candy melts
- Candy bracelets, unassembled
- Sugar pearls
- Edible silver luster spray

Tools

- Digital scale
- Sheet pans
- Microwave-safe bowls
- Lollipop sticks
- Toothpicks

1. Begin by hand weighing the cake into one-ounce portions. Shape the cake into rectangles and set them aside on a sheet pan. Place in the fridge while you prepare the candy melts.

2. Melt the white candy melts according to the directions indicated on the package. Add a few drops of the black candy color to get a light gray color.

3. Remove the cake from the fridge. Dip the sticks into the candy melts and insert them halfway into the cake.

4. Once the candy melts have fully set and the cake is back at room temperature, you are ready to dip the pops. Fully submerge the pops into the candy melts and tap off any excess. Set aside and allow to set in a stand.

5. While the pops are drying, glue a sugar pearl into the hole of the individual pieces of the candy that make up the candy bracelet to create ears. Allow the candy melts to set.

6. Once the pops are fully dry, place some of the gray candy melts created earlier into a plastic bag and snip off a corner. In the center of the pop, pipe the outline of a rectangle for the robot face. Around that rectangle, pipe lines in various positions to make it look as if the robot is made from metal panels. Add dots to represent the rivets and attach the ears. Allow to set in a stand.

7. When the melts have fully set, spray the pops with the silver luster in an even coat.

8. Melt both the black and green candy melts and place in plastic bags. Snip off the corners. With the black candy melts, flood the rectangle created earlier and allow it to set. Pipe on the eyes and mouth with green melts.

Sand Pail Cake Pops •••••••

Supplies

- Cake filling of your choice
- Red candy melts
- White candy melts
- Small yellow confetti sprinkles
- Peanuts

Tools

- Digital scale
- Sheet pans
- Microwave-safe bowls
- Lollipop sticks
- Plastic bags
- Pasta machine
- Food processor

1. Begin by hand weighing the cake into one-ounce portions. Roll them into balls and shape them to resemble buckets, with the bottom narrower than the top. Set aside on a sheet pan and place in the fridge while you prepare the candy melts and rim for the pails.

2. To create the rim of the pails, roll out fondant on the thickest setting on the pasta machine and cut them into ½ inch wide strips long enough to wrap around the top of the pops.

3. Melt the red candy melts according to the directions indicated on the package.

4. Remove the cake from the fridge. Dip the sticks into the candy melts and insert them halfway into the cake. Attach the fondant strips, using the candy melts, to the tops of the pops, making sure to have the fondant pass the tops of the cake in order to create a rim for the sand.

5. Once the candy melts and fondant have fully set and the cake is back at room temperature, you are ready to dip the pops. Fully submerge the pops into the candy melts and tap off any excess. Place the pops into a stand and allow them to fully dry.

6. While the pops are drying, crush the peanuts in a food processor until fine.

7. Once the pops are set, prepare the white candy melts in a plastic bag, snip the corner off, and pipe on the handles to the pails. While wet, attach a yellow confetti sprinkle on each side of the pops at the ends of the handles.

8. Pipe some candy melts into the rims of the pops and fill with the crushed peanuts.

Spade Cake Pops •••••••••

Supplies

- Cake filling of your choice
- White candy melts
- Black fondant
- Disco dust

Tools

- Digital scale
- Sheet pans
- Microwave-safe bowls
- Lollipop sticks
- Toothpicks
- Pasta machine
- 1¼ inch spade-shaped cookie cutter
- Stiff-bristle paintbrush

1. Begin by hand weighing the cake into one-ounce portions. Roll them into balls and set aside on a sheet pan. Place in the fridge while you prepare the candy melts.

2. Melt the white candy melts according to the directions indicated on the package.

3. Remove the cake balls from the fridge. Dip the sticks into the candy melts and insert them halfway into the cake balls.

4. Once the candy melts have fully set and the cake is back at room temperature, you are ready to dip the pops. Fully submerge the pops into the candy melts and tap off any excess. Place the pops into a stand and allow them to fully dry.

5. While the pops are drying, roll out the black fondant using the thickest setting on the pasta machine. Once the fondant has been rolled to an even thickness, dip the tip of the paintbrush into the jar of disco dust and tap it onto the fondant.

6. Using the cookie cutter, cut out the spade shapes. Use a toothpick to apply candy melts to the backs of them and attach them to the pops.

Variation

For a quick and simple variation try using different shapes, like hearts, diamonds, or even clubs.

Spool Cake Pops • • • • • • • • • • •

Supplies

- Cake filling of your choice
- Red candy melts
- Brown food color
- Vodka or lemon juice
- Fondant

Tools

- Digital scale
- Sheet pans
- Microwave-safe bowls
- Lollipop sticks
- Plastic bag
- Pasta machine
- Wood grain fondant impression mat
- 1½ inch circle cookie cutter
- Soft bristle paintbrush
- Straw

1. Roll out fondant ahead of time using the thickest setting on a pasta machine. Emboss the fondant with a wood grain impression mat. Cut out two circles using a small round cutter for each cake pop. Using a straw, cut a small circle out of the center of one circle of each pair. Allow to harden.

2. When the fondant has hardened, mix together a drop of vodka and brown food color. Paint the mixture onto the fondant with a soft-bristle paintbrush and allow to dry.

3. Hand weigh the cake into one-ounce portions. Roll them into logs, flattening the tops and bottoms. Make sure they are narrower than the fondant circles. Set aside on a sheet pan and place in the fridge while you prepare the candy melts.

4. Melt the red candy melts according to the directions indicated on the package. Remove the cake from the fridge. Dip the sticks into the candy melts and insert them halfway into the cake.

5. Once the candy melts have fully set and the cake is back at room temperature, the pops are ready to be dipped. Fully submerge the pops into the red candy melts and tap off any excess.

6. While still wet, slide on the bottom fondant circles and attach the top circles. Allow the candy melts to fully set.

7. In a small plastic bag melt the red candy melts, snip the corner off, and drizzle it on the center of the spools. Do it in layers, allowing each layer to set before moving on. This works best with thick candy melts.

Treasure Map Cake Pops • • •

Supplies

- Cake filling of your choice
- Peanut butter candy melts
- Red candy melts
- Green candy melts
- Blue candy melts
- Black candy melts
- Brown petal dust

Tools

- Digital scale
- Sheet pans
- Microwave-safe bowls
- Lollipop sticks
- Plastic bags
- Soft-bristle paintbrush
- Toothpicks

1. Begin by hand weighing the cake into one-ounce portions. Shape the cake into rectangles and flatten the tops with the palm of your hand. Don't worry if the cake edges crack when you flatten them.

2. Scratch the edges of the rectangles with a toothpick and lollipop stick to make it look as battered as possible.

3. Set them on a sheet pan and place in the fridge while you prepare the candy melts.

4. Melt the peanut butter candy melts according to the directions indicated on the package.

5. Remove the shaped cake from the fridge. Dip the sticks into the candy melts while holding the cake with fingers, both on top and underneath, and insert sticks halfway into the cake.

6. Once the candy melts have fully set and the cake is back at room temperature, you are ready to dip the pops. Fully submerge the pops into the candy melts and tap off any excess. Place the pops into a stand and allow them to fully dry.

7. When the pops are dry, dry dust them with brown petal dust, focusing mainly around the edges and anywhere you created a jagged surface to give the map an aged appearance.

8. Next prepare red, green, blue, black, and peanut butter melts in small plastic bags and cut off the tips of the bags.

9. Pipe a dotted line, trees, rocks, waves, and an X to mark the treasure spot onto the map.

Yellow Bear Cake Pops •••••

Supplies

- Cake filling of your choice
- Yellow candy melts
- Pink jumbo confetti sprinkles
- Purple jumbo confetti sprinkles
- Blue jumbo confetti sprinkles
- Black candy melts

Tools

- Digital scale
- Sheet pans
- Microwave-safe bowls
- Lollipop sticks
- Plastic bag

1. Begin by hand weighing the cake into one-ounce portions. Roll them into balls and press a jumbo confetti sprinkle against where the nose will be after being dipped, to create a flat surface. Set them aside on a sheet pan and place in the fridge while you prepare the candy melts.

2. Melt the yellow candy melts according to the directions indicated on the package.

3. Remove the cake balls from the fridge. Dip the sticks into the candy melts and insert them halfway into the cake balls.

4. Once the candy melts have fully set and the cake is back at room temperature, you are ready to dip the pops. Fully submerge the pops into the candy melts and tap off any excess.

5. While the pops are still wet, insert a pink and blue sprinkle for each ear, as well as a purple sprinkle in the indentation created earlier for the nose. Allow to fully set.

6. Prepare the black candy melts in a small plastic bag, snip off the corner, and pipe on dots for the eyes and nostrils.

Note

When working with a light color like yellow, remember to use a light-colored cake, as darker cakes will show through.

Variation

Dip your pops in white candy melts and use either all pink or all blue confetti sprinkles for the ears and noses to create bears perfect for a baby shower.

137

Garden

Bird Cage Cake Pops •••••••

Supplies

- Cake filling of your choice
- Pink candy melts
- White candy melts
- Green candy melts
- Orange candy melts
- Disco dust
- Small daisy sprinkles
- Light blue fondant
- Black edible marker

Tools

- Sheet pans
- Microwave-safe bowls
- Lollipop sticks
- Stiff-bristle paintbrush
- Toothpick
- Plastic bags
- Pasta machine
- 2¼ inch oval cookie cutter
- ¾ inch small rose petal cutter

1. Stuff the cookie cutter with the cake mixture, using the palm of your hand to squeeze out any excess cake. Gently push the cake out of the cookie cutter. Cut just under an inch off of the cake to create the basic bird cage shape. Chilling your dough ahead of time makes this process easier.

2. Set them aside on a sheet pan and place in the fridge while you prepare the candy melts.

3. Melt the pink candy melts according to the directions indicated on the package.

4. Remove the cake from the fridge. Dip the sticks into the candy melts and insert them halfway into the cake.

5. Once the candy melts have fully set and the cake is back at room temperature, you are ready to dip the pops. Fully submerge the cake into the candy melts and tap off any excess.

6. While still wet, with a dry paintbrush pick up disco dust, gently tap it over the pops, and allow to set.

7. In plastic bags melt both the white and green candy melts, snip off the corners, and pipe the outline of a bird cage with the white melts.

8. Once the white candy melts have set, pipe on vines with the green candy melts and attach daisy sprinkles to the vines. When the green melts have set, go back and pipe on little leaves, as well as dot white melts in the center of the daisies with a toothpick.

9. With a pasta machine, roll out the light fondant on the thickest setting and use a small rose petal cutter to cut out the body of the bird. With a black edible marker, draw on the eyes and wings. Pipe on beaks with orange candy melts and attach to the bird cage.

Butterfly Cake Pops

Supplies

- Cake filling of your choice
- White candy melts
- Black candy melts
- Assorted colors of pearl dust

Tools

- Sheet pans
- Microwave-safe bowls
- Lollipop sticks
- Plastic bag
- Soft-bristle paintbrush
- 1½ x ¾ inch rounded butterfly cookie cutter

1. Stuff the cookie cutter with the cake mixture, using the palm of your hand to squeeze out any excess cake. Gently push the cake out of the cookie cutter. Chilling your dough ahead of time makes this process easier.

2. Set them aside on a sheet pan and place in the fridge while you prepare the candy melts.

3. Melt the white candy melts according to the directions indicated on the package.

4. Remove the cake from the fridge. Dip the sticks into the candy melts and insert them halfway into the cake at a slight angle.

5. Once the candy melts have fully set and the cake is back at room temperature, the pops are ready to be dipped. Fully submerge the pops into the white candy melts, tap off any excess, and allow to set.

6. Pick up a small amount of the pearl dust on the tip of the paintbrush and tap off as much as possible. Lightly go over the whole pop in a circular motion, focusing mainly on the edges and leaving a small amount of the center still white. Go back and dust only the edges to make them bolder and more pronounced.

7. Put the melted black candy melts in a small bag and snip off the corner. Pipe on a design for the wings as well as the body in the center of the pops.

Dragonfly Cake Pops · · · · · ·

Supplies

- Cake filling of your choice
- White candy melts
- Purple candy melts
- White jumbo heart sprinkles
- Silver luster dust

Tools

- Sheet pans
- Microwave-safe bowls
- Lollipop sticks
- Plastic bag
- Soft-bristle paintbrush
- 1½ x ¾ inch daisy cookie cutter

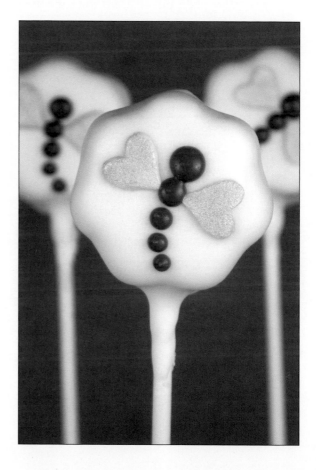

1. Stuff the cookie cutter with the cake mixture, using the palm of your hand to squeeze out any excess cake. Gently push the cake out of the cookie cutter. Chilling your dough ahead of time makes this process easier.

2. Set them aside on a sheet pan and place in the fridge while you prepare the candy melts.

3. Melt the white candy melts according to the directions indicated on the package.

4. Remove the cake from the fridge. Dip the sticks into the candy melts and insert them halfway into the cake.

5. Using a soft-bristle paintbrush, dry brush the hearts with silver luster dust until they are silver.

6. Once the candy melts have fully set and the cake is back at room temperature, the pops are ready to be dipped. Fully submerge the pops into the white candy melts and tap off any excess. While still wet, attach the hearts, leaving a small space between them. Allow to fully set in a stand.

7. Put the melted purple candy melts in a small plastic bag, cut off a corner, and pipe a series of dots for the body of the dragonfly. Tap the pop gently to smooth out the piped dots.

Garden Snake Cake Pops •••

Supplies

- Cake filling of your choice
- Green candy melts
- White candy melts
- Daisy sprinkles
- Edible markers
- Fondant
- Pink food color

Tools

- Digital scale
- Sheet pans
- Microwave-safe bowls
- Lollipop sticks
- Plastic bags

1. Begin by hand weighing the cake into one-ounce portions. Roll them into a ball and set them aside on a sheet pan. Place in the fridge while you prepare the candy melts.

2. Melt the green candy melts according to the directions indicated on the package.

3. Remove the cake balls from the fridge. Dip the sticks into the candy melts and insert them halfway into the cake.

4. Once the candy melts have fully set and the cake is back at room temperature, you are ready to dip the pops. Fully submerge the pops into the candy melts and tap off any excess.

5. While the pops are still wet, swirl the candy melts with a lollipop stick to add texture to the pop. Place them in a stand and allow them to fully set.

6. As the first coat of candy melts dries, prepare the snakes. Color the fondant using pink food color, pinch them into nickel-size portions, and roll them into the shape of a snake. With edible markers, draw various patterns onto the snakes and set them aside.

7. Dip a lollipop stick into the melted green candy melts and drab it around the pop, adding another textured layer on the pop. Attach both the snake and daisies onto the wet candy melts.

8. Once the candy melts have fully set, melt the white candy melts. Dip a toothpick into the white candy melts and dot on the center of the daisies.

Variation

Glue colored Sixlets onto the pop to create caterpillars.

Ladybug Cake Pops • • • • • • • •

Supplies

- Cake filling of your choice
- Red candy melts
- Black candy melts
- White confetti sprinkles

Tools

- Digital scale
- Sheet pans
- Microwave-safe bowls
- Lollipop sticks
- Plastic bag
- Toothpick

1. Begin by hand weighing the cake into one-ounce portions. Roll them into balls. Place a finger on the edge of each ball and roll to create a pear shape. Set aside on a sheet pan and place in the fridge while you prepare the candy melts.

2. Melt the red candy melts according to the directions indicated on the package.

3. Remove the cake from the fridge. Dip the sticks into the candy melts and insert them halfway into the cake at an angle.

4. Once the candy melts have fully set, and as the cake is back at room temperature, the pops are ready to be dipped. Fully submerge the pops into the red candy melts and tap off any excess. Allow to set in a stand.

5. Melt black candy melts according to the directions indicated on the package. Setting some aside for the head, fill a plastic bag with the black candy melts and snip off a small corner. Pipe a line of the candy melts down the center of the pop and immediately dip the head portion into the black melts.

6. Once the candy melts have set, pipe spots onto the bodies as well as two small dots on the heads to attach the white sprinkles. Attach the sprinkles and let set. Once set, pipe dots onto the eyes with the black candy melts.

Note

Do not melt the black candy melts for dipping and piping separately. If they are melted separately, the candy melts will be at two different temperatures and will cause a streaky finish on the head of the pop.

Potted Plants Cake Pops ...

Supplies

- Cake filling of your choice
- Red candy melts
- Orange candy melts
- Chocolate candy melts
- Green fondant
- Oreos

Tools

- Digital scale
- Sheet pans
- Microwave-safe bowls
- Lollipop sticks
- Plastic bags
- Pasta machine
- Food processor
- $7/_8$ inch leaf plunger

1. Begin by hand weighing the cake into one-ounce portions. Roll them into balls and shape them to resemble buckets with the bottoms narrower than the tops are. Set aside on a sheet pan and place in the fridge while you prepare the candy melts, the rim for the pails, and the plants.

2. To create the rim of the pails, roll out fondant on the thickest setting on the pasta machine and cut them into ½ wide strips long enough to wrap around the top of the pops.

3. Roll out the green fondant and cut out two leaves for each pop. Place the leaves on top of each other so that the veins are on the inside. Pinch the rounded ends together to create a stem and spread the leaves. Set them upside down to dry so the leaves are resting on a flat surface and the stem is in the air.

4. Melt the red, orange, and chocolate candy melts according to the directions indicated on the package. Blend together to achieve a terracotta color.

5. Remove the cake from the fridge. Dip the sticks into the candy melts and insert them halfway into the cake. Attach the fondant strips, using the candy melts, to the tops of the pops, making sure to have the fondant pass the top of the cake in order to create a rim to hold the dirt.

6. Once the candy melts have fully set, the fondant is attached, and the cake is back at room temperature, you are ready to dip the pops. Fully submerge the pops into the candy melts and tap off any excess. Place the pops into a stand and allow them to fully dry.

7. While the pops are drying, crush the Oreos in a food processor until fine.

8. Once the pops are set, pipe some chocolate candy melts into the rims of the pops and sprinkle with crushed Oreos. Insert the plants and allow to set.

Nature

Bear Cake Pops • • • • • • • • • • •

Supplies

- Cake filling of your choice
- Peanut butter candy melts
- Black candy melts
- Smarties

Tools

- Digital scale
- Sheet pans
- Microwave-safe bowls
- Lollipop sticks
- Plastic bags
- Toothpicks

1. Begin by hand weighing the cake into one-ounce portions. Roll them into balls with slight protrusions where the snout of the bear would be and add two indentations for the eyes using the tip of a lollipop stick. Set them aside on a sheet pan and place in the fridge while you prepare the candy melts.

2. Melt the peanut butter candy melts according to the directions indicated on the package.

3. Remove the cake balls from the fridge. Dip the sticks into the candy melts and insert them halfway into the cake balls. Dip two Smarties into the melts and attach at the top of the cake balls for the ears.

4. Once the candy melts have fully set and the cake is back at room temperature, you are ready to dip the pops. Fully submerge the pops into the candy melts and tap off any excess.

5. While the pops are still wet, take a toothpick and dab it up and down all around the pops. As the candy melts, fur-like texture will be created. Once set, add more candy melts with the toothpick and keep dabbing around until the desired fur results are achieved.

6. Prepare the black candy melts in a small plastic bag, snip off a small corner, and pipe on the eyes where the indentations were created, as well as the noses and mouths of the bears.

Cloud Cake Pops • • • • • • • • • •

Supplies

- Cake filling of your choice
- Light blue candy melts
- Royal icing

Tools

- Digital scale
- Sheet pans
- Microwave-safe bowls
- Lollipop sticks
- Piping bag
- #3 piping tip

1. Begin by hand weighing the cake into one-ounce portions. Roll them into balls and set them aside on a sheet pan. Place in the fridge while you prepare the candy melts.

2. Melt the light blue candy melts according to the directions indicated on the package.

3. Remove the cake balls from the fridge. Dip the sticks into the candy melts and insert them halfway into the cake balls.

4. Once the candy melts have fully set and the cake is back at room temperature, you are ready to dip the pops. Fully submerge the pops into the chocolate and tap off any excess. Place the pops into a stand and allow them to fully dry.

5. While the pops are drying, prepare the royal icing to medium consistency. The icing should be firm enough to hold its shape but soft enough to use a #3 piping tip.

6. Once the candy melts have fully set, randomly pipe on clouds all around the pops. Allow the pops to air for at least two hours so that the royal icing can harden.

Note

You can use melted white chocolate in place of the royal icing, but it will create flat clouds.

Variation

To create a night sky, dip the pops in dark blue candy melts and while still wet sprinkle with silver or gold disco dust. Allow to set before piping on clouds.

Mushroom Cake Pops ● ● ● ● ● ●

Supplies

- Cake filling of your choice
- White candy melts
- Black candy melts
- Red candy melts
- Green candy melts
- Small daisy sprinkles
- Small white confetti sprinkles

Tools

- Digital scale
- Sheet pans
- Microwave-safe bowls
- Lollipop sticks
- Toothpicks
- Plastic bag
- Stiff-bristle paintbrush

1. Begin by hand weighing the cake into one-ounce portions. Divide each into two separate portions, one weighing .30 ounces and the other .70 ounces. Roll the smaller cake portion into the shape of a teardrop, with a flat top instead of a pointed tip. For the larger cake, roll and shape it into a cone with a slight curve to the tip. Set them aside on a sheet pan and place in the fridge while you prepare the candy melts.

2. Melt the white and black candy melts according to the directions indicated on the package.

3. Remove the cake from the fridge. Using a stiff-bristle paintbrush, paint the black candy melts onto the flat side of the mushroom cap. Brush in even strokes all the way around the cap and in layers to create the texture of the gills. Dip the sticks into the white candy melts and insert them completely through the stem of the mushroom, exposing the stick.

4. Once the candy melts have fully set and your cake is back at room temperature, you are ready to dip the pops. Fully submerge the stem of the pop into the white candy melts and tap off any excess. Once all the excess has been tapped off, place the cap onto the stem and allow to set.

5. Melt the red candy melts according to the directions indicated on the package. Dip the caps of the pops in the melted red candy melts so they slightly overlap the gills of the mushroom. Set back into the stand to dry.

6. When the caps have dried, dot on white candy melts with a toothpick and attach white confetti sprinkles.

7. Place the melted green candy melts in a plastic bag, snip off the corner of the bag, and pipe strands of grass on the base. While still wet, attach daisy sprinkles to the grass.

Variation

For a more natural mushroom, follow the same basic steps, but use a rounded tablespoon as a mold to create the cap of the mushroom and dip it in chocolate candy melts. When the pop is dry, dry dust it with brown and green petal dust for a rustic look.

Owl Cake Pops ● ● ● ● ● ● ● ● ● ● ●

Supplies

- Cake filling of your choice
- White candy melts
- Pink candy melts
- Rainbow-chip sprinkles
- Pink jumbo heart sprinkles
- Small pink confetti sprinkles
- Orange candy-coated sunflower seeds
- Orange star sprinkles
- Fondant

Tools

- Digital scale
- Sheet pans
- Microwave-safe bowls
- Lollipop sticks
- Plastic bags
- Toothpicks
- ⁵/₈ inch circle fondant cutter
- Pasta machine

1. Begin by hand weighing the cake into one-ounce portions. Roll them into an oval shape and set them aside on a sheet pan. Place them in the fridge for a few minutes while you prepare the candy melts.

2. Melt the white candy melts according to the directions indicated on the package.

3. Remove the cake from the fridge. Dip the sticks into the candy melts and insert them halfway into the cake. Attach two rainbow-chip sprinkles, using candy melts, to the top of the pops for the ears.

4. Once the candy melts have fully set on the ears and where the stick was inserted, you are ready to dip the pops. Allow the pops to come to room temperature before dipping. Fully submerge the pops into the candy melts and tap off any excess. Place the pops into a stand and allow to fully dry.

5. While the pops are drying, melt the pink candy melts according to the directions indicated on the package. Once the pops are dry, dip then again in the pink candy melts in a diagonal direction, covering both ears and creating a white triangular belly.

6. As the second coat of candy melts is drying, prepare the eyes. Roll out fondant on the thickest pasta machine setting and cut out circles. Set them aside until needed.

7. Take some of the white candy melts from earlier and place in a small plastic bag. Snip off the corner of the bag and, on the belly of the owl, pipe a series of swags going across the white portion of the pop. Allow to set.

8. Use a toothpick to dot on melted candy melts and attach the eyes just above the point of the white triangle. Once set, attach pink confetti sprinkles to the eyes and allow to set before you dot on melted black candy melts.

9. Between the eyes add a dot of candy melts and glue on the candy-coated sunflower seeds as the beak.

10. Attach two heart-shaped sprinkles and a confetti sprinkle to the top of the owl with the candy melts, just below the ear, for the bow.

11. Attach the orange stars to the body of the owl for the feet.

Variation

To create a more authentic owl, follow the same steps as above but dip the body in peanut butter melts for the base and chocolate melts for the top coat. Use yellow confetti sprinkles for the eyes for more of a wild effect. Dip mini pretzel sticks in chocolate to create tree branches for the bottom of the owls.

Pets

Cat Cake Pops •••••••••••

Supplies

- Cake filling of your choice
- Black candy melts
- Yellow candy melts
- White candy melts
- Yellow jumbo confetti sprinkles
- Jumbo heart sprinkles
- White Sixlets

Tools

- Digital scale
- Sheet pans
- Microwave-safe bowls
- Lollipop sticks
- Plastic bags
- Toothpicks

1. Begin by hand weighing the cake into one-ounce portions. Roll them into balls and set aside on a sheet pan. Place in the fridge while you prepare the candy melts.

2. Melt the black candy melts according to the directions indicated on the package.

3. Remove the cake balls from the fridge. Dip the sticks into the candy melts and insert them halfway into the cake balls.

4. Use the jumbo heart sprinkles for the ears. Slightly dip the rounded portion of the hearts into the candy melts and insert into the cake. Take two white Sixlets and use them to create an indentation in the cake where they will be placed after being dipped. You want to position them on the lower portion of the cake ball, just under where you plan on adding the nose.

5. Once the candy melts have fully set on the ears, you are ready to dip the pops. Allow the pops to come to room temperature before dipping. Fully submerge the pops into the candy melts and tap off any excess, keeping the face of the pop towards you. Once the excess candy melts have been removed, while still wet, place two white Sixlets into the indentations created earlier. If the candy melts pool up around where you placed them, gently tap the pops on the edge of your dipping vessel to smooth it out once again.

6. Place the pops in a stand and allow them to fully dry. Once dry, dot the eyes onto the pop with the melted black candy melts. Glue on jumbo confetti sprinkles and let the pops set.

7. Place a small amount of melted white, yellow, and black candy melts in separate plastic bags. Snip off corners of the bags and set aside until needed.

8. Using the black candy melts, pipe the pupils of the eyes as well as dots onto the Sixlets and let set. Once set, take the yellow melts and pipe a nose between the two Sixlets and allow to set.

9. Dot white candy melts onto the pupils of the eyes.

Dog Cake Pops

Supplies

- Cake filling of your choice
- Chocolate candy melts
- Black candy melts
- Red candy melts

Tools

- Sheet pans
- Microwave-safe bowls
- Lollipop sticks
- Plastic bags
- 2 x ¾ inch dog cookie cutter

1. Stuff the cookie cutter with the cake mixture, using the palm of your hand to squeeze out any excess cake. Gently push the cake out of the cookie cutter. Chilling your dough ahead of time makes this process easier.

2. Set them aside on a sheet pan and place in the fridge while you prepare the candy melts.

3. Melt the chocolate candy melts according to the directions indicated on the package.

4. Remove the shaped cake from the fridge. Dip the sticks into the candy melts while holding the cake with fingers, both on top and underneath, and insert sticks halfway into the cake.

5. Once the candy melts have fully set and the cake is back at room temperature, you are ready to dip the pops. Fully submerge the pops into the candy melts and tap off any excess. Place them in a stand and allow them to fully set.

6. Once the pops are fully dried, fill a small plastic bag with the chocolate candy melts and snip off a small piece of the corner. Pipe small strands of fur, leaving space between each strand, starting at the base of the pop. Allow to set and fill in the spaces you created with more strands of chocolate. Repeat in layers until the whole pop is fully covered.

7. Place both the melted red and black candy melts in plastic bags for piping. Using the black candy melts, dot an eye and nose onto the pop. With the red candy melts, pipe on a collar around the neck.

Dog Dish Cake Pops · · · · · · ·

Supplies

- Cake filling of your choice
- Red candy melts
- Black candy melts
- Chocolate candy melts
- Sugar pearls
- Bone candies

Tools

- Digital scale
- Sheet pans
- Microwave-safe bowls
- Lollipop sticks
- Plastic bag

1. Begin by hand weighing the cake into one-ounce portions. Shape them as cones with flat tops to create the shape of dog dishes. Set aside on a sheet pan and place in the fridge while you prepare the candy melts.

2. Melt the red candy melts according to the directions indicated on the package. Remove the cake from the fridge. Dip the sticks into the candy melts and insert them halfway into the cake.

3. Once the candy melts have fully set and the cake is back at room temperature, the pops are ready to be dipped. Fully submerge the pops into the red candy melts and tap off any excess. Allow to set in a stand.

4. Fill a plastic bag with the black candy melts and snip off a small corner. Pipe a name on the front of the dishes and paws on the opposite sides of the name. Allow to fully set.

5. Melt the chocolate candy melts. Fill a small bowl with sugar pearls and pour the candy melts over them so that all the pearls are evenly coated.

6. Place a small amount of the chocolate-covered sugar pearls on top of the dishes with a spoon and attach the bones while still wet.

Fish Bone Cake Pops • • • • • • •

Supplies

- Cake filling of your choice
- White candy melts
- Black candy melts

Tools

- Digital scale
- Sheet pans
- Microwave-safe bowls
- Lollipop sticks
- Plastic bag
- Toothpick
- 1⅞ x ¾ inch fish cookie cutter

1. Stuff the cookie cutter with the cake mixture, using the palm of your hand to squeeze out any excess cake. Gently push the cake out of the cookie cutter. Chilling your dough ahead of time makes this process easier.

2. Set them aside on a sheet pan and place in the fridge while you prepare the candy melts.

3. Melt the white candy melts according to the directions indicated on the package.

4. Remove the cake from the fridge. Dip the sticks into the candy melts and insert them halfway into the cake.

5. Once the candy melts have fully set and the cake is back at room temperature, the pops are ready to be dipped. Fully submerge the pops into the candy melts, tap off any excess, and allow to set.

6. When the pops have set, prepare the black candy melts in a plastic bag and snip off the corners. Pipe fish skeletons on top. Dot the heads with white candy melts, using a toothpick to create an eye socket.

Fish Cake Pops • • • • • • • • • • • •

Supplies

- Cake filling of your choice
- Light blue candy melts
- Green candy melts
- Black candy melts
- Blue pearl dust

Tools

- Digital scale
- Sheet pans
- Microwave-safe bowls
- Lollipop sticks
- Plastic bags
- Stiff-bristle paintbrush
- Soft-bristle paintbrush
- 1⅞ x ¾ inch fish cookie cutter

1. Stuff the cookie cutter with the cake mixture, using the palm of your hand to squeeze out any excess cake. Gently push the cake out of the cookie cutter. Chilling your dough ahead of time makes this process easier.

2. Set them aside on a sheet pan and place in the fridge while you prepare the candy melts.

3. Melt the light blue candy melts according to the directions indicated on the package.

4. Remove the cake from the fridge. Dip the sticks into the light blue candy melts and insert them halfway into the cake.

5. Once the candy melts have fully set and the cake is back at room temperature, the pops are ready to be dipped. Fully submerge the pops into the light blue candy melts, tap off any excess, and allow to set.

6. Prepare the green and black candy melts in small plastic bags and snip the corners off. With the green melts pipe a line on the top, tail, and bottom fins. Brush on the candy melts with the stiff-bristle paintbrush to create the illusion of a fin. Once that sets, pipe on the scales. Use the black melts to pipe on an eye and a mouth.

7. Once the candy melts have fully set, dry dust the pops with a blue pearl dust with a soft-bristle paintbrush.

Sports

Basketball Cake Pops • • • • • •

Supplies

- Cake filling of your choice
- Orange candy melts
- Black candy melts

Tools

- Digital scale
- Sheet pans
- Microwave-safe bowls
- Lollipop sticks
- Plastic bags

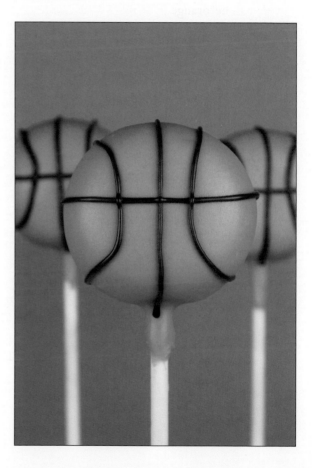

1. Begin by hand weighing the cake into one-ounce portions. Roll them into a ball and flatten the tops of them until you have a rounded, flat circle. Set them aside on a sheet pan and place in the fridge while you prepare the candy melts.

2. Melt the orange candy melts according to the directions indicated on the package.

3. Remove the cake from the fridge. Dip the sticks into the candy melts and insert them halfway into the cake.

4. Once the candy melts have fully set and the cake is back at room temperature, you are ready to dip the pops. Fully submerge the pops into the candy melts and tap off any excess. Place in a stand and allow to set.

5. Place the melted black candy melts in a plastic bag and snip off a corner. Pipe on the basketball lines and allow to set.

Variation

Follow the same basic steps to create baseballs and tennis and soccer balls.

Note

Although you can do the basketballs or any sports ball as a rounded pop, it is much easier to pipe on straight lines if you are working with a flat surface.

Bowling Ball Cake Pops • • • • •

Supplies

- Cake filling of your choice
- Purple candy melts
- White candy melts
- Black candy melts
- Pink luster dust

Tools

- Digital scale
- Sheet pans
- Microwave-safe bowls
- Lollipop sticks
- Plastic bags
- Soft-bristle paintbrush

1. Begin by hand weighing the cake into one-ounce portions. Roll them into balls and set aside on a sheet pan. Place in the fridge while you prepare the candy melts.

2. Melt the purple and white candy melts according to the directions indicated on the package.

3. Remove the cake from the fridge. Dip the sticks into the candy melts and insert them halfway into the cake.

4. Once the candy melts have fully set and the cake is back at room temperature, you are ready to dip the pops.

5. To achieve the marble effect, drizzle white candy melts on top of the purple candy melts. Fully submerge the pops into the candy melts and rotate while pulling up and tapping off any excess. For each pop dipped, drizzle new white candy melts on top of the purple melts. Place the pops into a stand and allow them to fully dry.

6. Once the pops are dried, dry dust them with the pink luster dust.

7. Prepare the black candy melts in a plastic bag, snip off the corner, and pipe three dots onto each pop.

Note

You can do the marble technique with different colors, but it is easier if one of the colors is white to prevent mixing.

Bowling Pin Cake Pops •••••

Supplies

- Cake filling of your choice
- White candy melts
- Red candy melts

Tools

- Digital scale
- Sheet pans
- Microwave-safe bowls
- Lollipop sticks
- Plastic bags

1. Begin by hand weighing the cake into one-ounce portions. Roll them into balls and sculpt them to resemble bowling pins. Set aside on a sheet pan and place in the fridge while you prepare the candy melts.

2. Melt the white candy melts according to the directions indicated on the package.

3. Remove the cake from the fridge. Dip the sticks into the candy melts and insert them halfway into the cake.

4. Once the candy melts have fully set and the cake is back at room temperature, you are ready to dip the pops. Fully submerge the pops into the candy melts and tap off any excess. Place the pops into a stand and allow them to fully dry.

5. While the pops are drying, place the melted red candy melts in a small plastic bag and cut off the tip of the bag.

6. Once the pops are dried, pipe two stripes around the neck of the pins and allow to set.

Sweets & Treats

Chocolate Chip Cookie Cake Pops ● ● ● ● ● ● ● ● ● ● ● ● ● ● ● ●

Supplies

- Cake filling of your choice
- Peanut butter candy melts
- Chocolate candy melts
- Brown petal dust

Tools

- Digital scale
- Sheet pans
- Microwave-safe bowls
- Lollipop sticks
- Plastic bag
- Soft-bristle paintbrush
- Aluminum foil

1. Begin by hand weighing the cake into one-ounce portions. Roll them into balls and, with the palm of your hand, flatten them to resemble cookies. Take a piece of aluminum foil and crumple it into a compact ball. Roll the ball of foil all over the cake to create the baked texture.

2. Set them aside on a sheet pan and place in the fridge while you prepare the candy melts.

3. Melt the peanut butter and chocolate candy melts according to the directions indicated on the package. Place the chocolate candy melts in a small plastic bag, snip off the corner, and set aside for use later.

4. Remove the cake from the fridge. Dip the sticks into the candy melts and insert them halfway into the cake.

5. When the cake is ready to dip, fully submerge the pops into the candy melts and tap off any excess. Once the excess has been fully tapped off, randomly pipe on the melted chocolate for chocolate chips. Allow the pops to fully set.

6. Once the pops have fully set, dry dust the whole pop with brown petal dust to create a baked look, focusing mainly around the edges.

Cinnamon Roll Cake Pops •••

Supplies

- Cake filling of your choice
- Peanut butter candy melts
- Brown petal dust
- Royal icing
- Cinnamon

Tools

- Digital scale
- Sheet pans
- Microwave-safe bowls
- Lollipop sticks
- Soft-bristle paintbrush

1. Begin by hand weighing the cake into one-ounce portions. Roll them into balls and, with the palm of your hand, flatten them slightly. Take a lollipop stick and, starting near the bottom, press it against each cake to create a spiral indentation. The indentations will look rough and will need to be softened with your fingertips. Set cakes aside on a sheet pan and place in the fridge while you prepare the candy melts and royal icing.

2. Melt the peanut butter candy melts according to the directions indicated on the package.

3. Remove the cake from the fridge. Dip the sticks into the peanut butter candy melts and insert them halfway into the cake.

4. While the candy melts set and the cake returns to room temperature, prepare the royal icing to a flooding consistency. When the cake is ready to dip, fully submerge the pops into the candy melts and tap off any excess. Allow to set in a stand.

5. Once the pops have fully set, lightly dry dust the whole pop with brown petal dust to create a baked look. Focus the dust heavily around the spiral to make it darker than the rest of the pop.

6. When you finish dusting, apply a small amount of royal icing on top and tap the pop to make it spread out. Sprinkle on cinnamon and allow the royal icing to fully set.

Frosted Sugar Cookie Cake Pops ● ● ● ● ● ● ● ● ● ● ● ● ●

Supplies

- Cake filling of your choice
- White candy melts
- Light blue candy melts
- Nonpareils
- Yellow color dust
- Brown color dust

Tools

- Digital scale
- Sheet pans
- Microwave-safe bowls
- Lollipop sticks
- Soft-bristle paintbrush
- Small pallet knife

1. Begin by hand weighing the cake into one-ounce portions. Roll them into balls and slightly flatten on top. Set aside on a sheet pan and place in the fridge while you prepare the candy melts.

2. Melt the white and light blue candy melts according to the directions indicated on the package.

3. Remove the cake from the fridge. Dip the sticks into the white candy melts and insert them halfway into the cake.

4. Once the candy melts have fully set and the cake is back at room temperature, the pops are ready to be dipped. Fully submerge the pops into the white candy melts and tap off any excess. Allow to fully set in a stand.

5. Once the candy melts have set, lightly dust the pops with the brown and yellow dust to give them a light golden color.

6. Allow the light blue candy melts to cool as much as possible, stirring occasionally until they reach the consistency of a thick frosting. Using a small pallet knife, frost the top of the pop and sprinkle on the nonpareils. If the candy melts fully cool before the sprinkles can stick, quickly pass the pop over a low open flame to soften the candy melts. Allow the pops to set.

Note

If you want to avoid dry dusting the pops, use peanut butter candy melts and white chocolate to achieve the proper tone.

Gumdrop Cake Pops ·······

Supplies

- Cake filling of your choice
- Candy melts of your choice
- Sanding sugar of your choice

Tools

- Digital scale
- Sheet pans
- Microwave-safe bowls
- Lollipop sticks

1. Begin by hand weighing the cake into one-ounce portions. Shape them to look like gumdrops and set them aside on a sheet pan. Place in the fridge while you prepare the candy melts.

2. Melt the colored candy melts of your choosing according to the directions indicated on the package.

3. Remove the shaped cake from the fridge. Dip the sticks into the candy melts and insert them halfway into the cake.

4. Once the candy melts have fully set and the cake is back at room temperature, you are ready to dip the pops. Fully submerge the pops into the candy melts and tap off any excess.

5. While the pops are still wet, pour the sanding sugar over the pop to cover any exposed candy melts. Use the same colored sugar as the candy melts used.

6. Place them in a stand and allow them to fully set.

Jawbreaker Cake Pops • • • • •

Supplies

- Cake filling of your choice
- White candy melts
- Red food coloring
- Green food coloring
- Yellow food coloring
- Blue food coloring
- Vodka or lemon juice

Tools

- Digital scale
- Sheet pans
- Microwave-safe bowls
- Lollipop sticks
- Stiff-bristle paintbrush

1. Begin by hand weighing the cake into one-ounce portions. Roll them into balls and set aside on a sheet pan. Place in the fridge while you prepare the candy melts.

2. Melt the white candy melts according to the directions indicated on the package.

3. Remove the cake balls from the fridge. Dip the sticks into the candy melts and insert them halfway into the cake balls.

4. Once the candy melts have fully set and the cake is back at room temperature, you are ready to dip the pops. Fully submerge the pops into the candy melts and tap off any excess. Place in a stand and allow them to fully dry.

5. Mix together small amounts of each food coloring with vodka or lemon juice. Dip the tip of a stiff-bristle paintbrush in the food coloring and flick the bristles with your fingertip to fling the colors onto the pops.

6. Allow the food color on the pops to fully dry.

Note

Using water-based food coloring is ideal as it will dry without remaining tacky like gel- and oil-based colors do. Also try using bright white candy melts to allow the colors to pop.

Pancake Cake Pops ● ● ● ● ● ● ● ●

Supplies

- Cake filling of your choice
- Peanut butter candy melts
- Chocolate candy melts
- Brown petal dust
- Yellow fondant

Tools

- Digital scale
- Sheet pans
- Microwave-safe bowls
- Lollipop sticks
- Plastic bag
- Soft-bristle paintbrush
- Pasta machine

1. Begin by hand weighing the cake into one-ounce portions. Roll it into a log and cut it into three equal portions. Roll the three equal portions into balls and flatten them with the palm of your hand. Stack them together and lightly press down on the top of the stack. Set them aside on a sheet pan and place in the fridge while you prepare the candy melts.

2. Melt the peanut butter candy melts according to the directions indicated on the package.

3. Remove the cake from the fridge and add a drop of the peanut butter melts in between each layer of cake. Dip the sticks into the candy melts and insert them completely through the first two layers of cake and halfway through the third layer of cake.

4. Once the candy melts have fully set and the cake is back at room temperature, you are ready to dip the pops. Fully submerge the stems of the pops into the candy melts and tap off any excess. Place in a stand and allow to fully dry.

5. With a soft-bristle brush, lightly brush brown petal dust to give the pops a cooked look.

6. Roll out the fondant on the thickest setting of a pasta machine and cut out small squares. Set them aside and prepare the chocolate candy melts in a small plastic bag. Snip off the corner of the bag, pipe the chocolate candy melts on top, and allow to spill over the sides. While still wet, place the small yellow squares on top.

Peanut Cake Pops ·········

Supplies

- Cake filling of your choice
- Peanut butter candy melts
- Royal icing
- Brown petal dust

Tools

- Digital scale
- Sheet pans
- Microwave-safe bowls
- Lollipop sticks
- Piping bags
- #2 piping tip
- Soft-bristle paintbrush

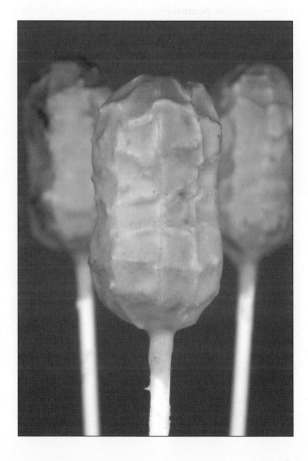

1. Begin by hand weighing the cake into one-ounce portions. Shape them to look like peanuts and set aside on a sheet pan. Place in the fridge while you prepare the candy melts and royal icing.

2. Melt the peanut butter candy melts according to the directions indicated on the package.

3. Remove the cake from the fridge. Dip the sticks into the candy melts and insert them halfway into the cake.

4. While the candy melts set and the cake comes back to room temperature, prepare the royal icing to medium consistency. The icing should be firm enough to hold its shape but soft enough to pipe using a #2 piping tip. Fill a piping bag fitted with a #2 tip with the royal icing. Pipe vertical lines going from the tops of the pops to the bases. Then pipe a series of randomly placed horizontal lines between the vertical ones. Allow the pops to sit for at least 10 minutes before dipping so the royal icing can harden slightly.

5. When the cake is ready to dip, fully submerge the pops into the candy melts, tap off any excess, and allow to set.

6. Once the pops have fully set, dry dust them with brown petal dust to highlight the craters.

Snow Cone Cake Pops ‧ ‧ ‧ ‧ ‧

Supplies

- Cake filling of your choice
- White candy melts
- Green sanding sugar
- Yellow sanding sugar
- Red sanding sugar
- Edible white sugar sheets

Tools

- Digital scale
- Sheet pans
- Microwave-safe bowls
- Lollipop sticks
- Stiff-bristle paintbrush

1. Begin by hand weighing the cake into one-ounce portions. Shape them into cones with rounded tops and set aside on a sheet pan. Place in the fridge while you prepare the candy melts.

2. Melt the white candy melts according to the directions indicated on the package.

3. Remove the cake from the fridge. Dip the sticks into the candy melts and insert them halfway into the cake.

4. Once the candy melts have fully set and the cake is back at room temperature, you are ready to dip the pops. Fully submerge the pops into the candy melts, tap off any excess, and allow to set.

5. When the pops have set, paint on the white candy melts around a third of the rounded top with a stiff-bristle paintbrush. Sprinkle on the red sanding sugar and let set. When the candy melts have hardened, repeat the steps for the remaining two colors.

6. Once all three colors has been added, to create the ice of the snow cone you will need to cut the edible white sugar sheets to wrap around the bases of the pops. Glue them in place with candy melts.

Special Occasions

Birthday Cake Pops · · · · · · ·

Supplies

- Cake filling of your choice
- White candy melts
- Blue candy melts
- Red fondant
- Mini confetti sprinkles
- Nonpareils

Tools

- Sheet pans
- Microwave-safe bowls
- Lollipop sticks
- Plastic bag
- Pasta machine
- 1½ x ¾ inch round cookie cutter
- ¾ inch numerical fondant cutters

1. Stuff the cookie cutter with the cake mixture, using the palm of your hand to squeeze out any excess cake. Gently push the cake out of the cookie cutter. Chilling your dough ahead of time makes this process easier.

2. Set them aside on a sheet pan and place in the fridge while you prepare the candy melts.

3. Melt the white candy melts according to the directions indicated on the package.

4. Remove the cake from the fridge. Dip the sticks into the candy melts and insert them halfway into the cake. Set on a stand to dry.

5. While the candy melts are drying and the cake comes to room temperature, roll out the fondant using a pasta machine on the thickest setting and cut out any number you wish.

6. When the cake is ready to dip, fully submerge the pops into the candy melts and tap off any excess. While still wet, place the fondant number in the center and sprinkle on the sprinkles. Allow to fully set.

7. Once the pops have fully set, in a small plastic bag place the melted blue candy melts and snip off the corner. Pipe a beaded boarder around the cake. It is best to use candy melts with a thicker consistency for this step.

Brush Embroidery
Cake Pops • • • • • • • • • • • • • • • •

Supplies

- Cake filling of your choice
- White candy melts
- Royal icing
- Food coloring

Tools

- Sheet pans
- Microwave-safe bowls
- Lollipop sticks
- Stiff-bristle paintbrush
- Piping bags
- #3 piping tip
- #2 piping tip
- Digital scale

1. Prepare a batch of royal icing, divide it in half, and color half using any food coloring. Fill a piping bag that has a #3 tip with the colored icing and set aside. With the remaining white icing, fill a piping bag fitted with a #2 piping tip.

2. Hand weigh the cake into one-ounce portions. Roll them into balls, set aside on a sheet pan, and place in the fridge while you prepare the candy melts.

3. Melt the white candy melts according to the directions indicated on the package. Remove the cake from the fridge. Dip the sticks into the candy melts and insert them halfway into the cake.

4. Once the candy melts have fully set and the cake is back at room temperature, the pops are ready to be dipped. Fully submerge the pops into the white candy melts and tap off any excess. Set aside to fully dry.

5. Once the pops have dried, pipe four curved lines with the colored icing for the outline of a flower. Before the icing hardens, drag it inwards toward the center of the flower with the paintbrush. Pipe smaller curved lines for another layer of petals and repeat. Once you have piped and created a few flowers, dot the centers of each flower and pipe a swirl next to each one. Allow the icing to fully harden before covering.

Pink Floral Cake Pops • • • • • •

Supplies

- Cake filling of your choice
- Pink candy melts
- White candy melts
- Sugar pearls
- Disco dust
- Pink pearl dust
- Fondant

Tools

- Impression mat
- Digital scale
- Sheet pans
- Microwave-safe bowls
- Lollipop sticks
- Plastic bag
- Toothpick
- Stiff-bristle paintbrush
- Pasta machine
- 1 inch flower plunger

1. Roll out fondant ahead of time using the thickest setting on a pasta machine. Cut out flowers using the flower plunger, pressing firmly into the impression mat. Set aside and let dry.

2. Once the fondant flowers are dry, using a small paintbrush dust the centers with the pink pearl dust. Melt some white candy melts and add a dot of it to the center of the flowers with a toothpick. Attach a sugar pearl and allow to set.

3. Hand weigh the cake into one-ounce portions. Roll them into balls and set aside on a sheet pan. Place in the fridge while you prepare the candy melts.

4. Melt the pink candy melts according to the directions indicated on the package.

5. Remove the cake from the fridge. Dip the sticks into the candy melts and insert them halfway into the cake.

6. Once the candy melts have fully set and the cake is back at room temperature, the pops are ready to be dipped. Fully submerge the pops into the pink candy melts and tap off any excess.

7. While still wet, dust the tops with disco dust by tapping the paintbrush onto the pops. Allow to set in a stand.

8. In a small plastic bag, place the melted white candy melts, snip the corner off, pipe on top four swirls, and attach the fondant flowers to the center.

Wedding Cake Pops　• • • • • • • •

Supplies

- Cake filling of your choice
- White candy melts
- Pink fondant
- Green fondant

Tools

- Pasta machine
- Sheet pans
- Microwave-safe bowls
- Lollipop sticks
- Plastic bag
- 1½ x ¾ inch medium-size round cookie cutter
- ⅝ x ¾ inch small-size round cookie cutter
- 2¼ inch square cookie cutter
- ⅞ inch leaf plunger

208

1. Stuff the round cookie cutters with the cake mixture, using the palm of your hand to squeeze out any excess cake. Gently push the cake out of the cookie cutters. Chilling your dough ahead of time makes this process easier.

2. Set them aside on a sheet pan and place in the fridge while you prepare the candy melts.

3. Melt the white candy melts according to the directions indicated on the package.

4. Remove the cake from the fridge. Dip the sticks into the candy melts and insert them completely through the larger circles, exposing at least ¼ of the sticks. Dip the tip of the sticks into the candy melts then attach the smaller round circle on top.

5. While the candy melts are drying and the cake comes to room temperature, roll out the pink and green fondant using a pasta machine. For each pop, cut out two leaves using the leaf plunger. Cut squares out of the pink fondant using the square cookie cutter and cut each into ¾ inch wide stripes. Fold the strips in half horizontally and roll to create a rose. Set aside.

6. When the cake is ready to dip, fully submerge the pops into the candy melts and tap off any excess. Allow to fully set.

7. Once the pops have fully set, in a small plastic bag prepare the white candy melts and snip off the corner. Pipe swags around the top and bottom tiers. Once the swags have dried, pipe a beaded border around the edges of both tiers. Using thicker consistency melts works best for this.

8. Once the candy melts have set, attach the leaves and rose to the tops of the pops.

Under the Sea

Clam Cake Pops · · · · · · · · · · ·

Supplies

- Cake filling of your choice
- Peanut butter candy melts
- Green candy melts
- Pink candy melts
- Gold luster dust
- Silver luster dust
- Fondant
- White Sixlets
- Almonds

Tools

- Digital scale
- Sheet pans
- Microwave-safe bowls
- Lollipop sticks
- Plastic bags
- Soft-bristle paintbrush
- Wax paper
- Food processor
- Clam fondant mold

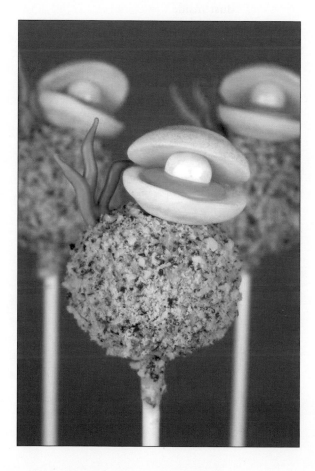

1. Prepare the clam shells ahead of time. Press the fondant into the clam fondant mold and create two pieces per pop.

2. Lightly dust the shells with gold luster dust and set aside to harden. Place the Sixlets and silver luster dust inside a small plastic bag. Shake the bag until the Sixlets are fully covered.

3. Melt the pink and green candy in a small plastic bag and snip off the corners. Pipe strands of seaweed on wax paper with the green melts and allow to harden. Using the pink melts, flood the inside of one shell and add a Sixlet to it while wet. Brush a line of water at the back hinge of the shell with a paintbrush and attach the upper shell.

4. In a food processor finely grind the almonds.

5. Hand weigh the cake into one-ounce portions. Roll them into balls and set aside on a sheet pan. Place in the fridge while you prepare the candy melts.

6. Melt the peanut butter candy melts according to the directions indicated on the package.

7. Remove the cake from the fridge. Dip the sticks into the candy melts and insert them halfway into the cake.

8. Once the candy melts have fully set and the cake is back at room temperature, the pops are ready to be dipped. Fully submerge the pops into the peanut butter candy melts and tap off any excess.

9. While still wet, sprinkle the crushed almonds all over the pop, covering any exposed candy melts. Insert and attach the seaweed created earlier. Allow to fully set.

10. Once the pops have hardened, attach the clam shells to the tops of the pops with candy melts.

Coral Cake Pops

Supplies

- Cake filling of your choice
- Light blue candy melts
- Orange candy melts
- Green candy melts
- Yellow candy melts
- Pink candy melts
- Purple candy melts
- Red candy melts
- Peanuts

Tools

- Digital scale
- Sheet pans
- Microwave-safe bowls
- Lollipop sticks
- Plastic bags
- Food processor

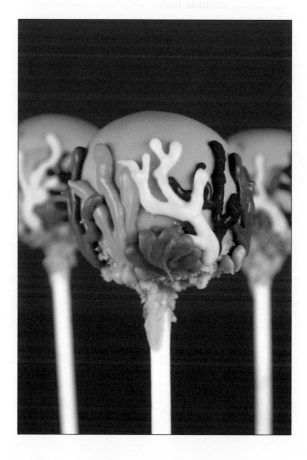

1. Begin by hand weighing the cake into one-ounce portions. Roll them into a ball and set them aside on a sheet pan. Place in the fridge while you prepare the candy melts.

2. Melt the light blue candy melts according to the directions indicated on the package.

3. Remove the cake balls from the fridge. Dip the sticks into the candy melts and insert them halfway into the cake balls and set aside.

4. In a food processor chop up the peanuts to a fine, sand-like grain.

5. Once the candy melts have fully set and the cake is back at room temperature, you are ready to dip the pops. Fully submerge the pops into the candy melts and tap off any excess.

6. While the pops are still wet, invert the pop so that the stick is up in the air and sprinkle the chopped peanuts on the bottom of the ball for the sand. Allow to fully set.

7. Prepare the various colored candy melts in small plastic bags, snip off the corners, and pipe on a variety of coral designs using the different colors. Using a thicker chocolate is best for this.

Note

If you are afraid of inverting the pops while still wet you can brush on melted blue candy melts when dry to add the peanuts.

Life Preserver Cake Pops ● ● ●

Supplies

- Cake filling of your choice
- Light blue candy melts
- Life Savers mints
- Red edible marker

Tools

- Digital scale
- Sheet pans
- Microwave-safe bowls
- Lollipop sticks

1. Begin by hand weighing the cake into one-ounce portions. Roll them into a ball and set them aside on a sheet pan. Place in the fridge while you prepare the candy melts.

2. Melt the light blue candy melts according to the directions indicated on the package.

3. Remove the cake balls from the fridge. Dip the sticks into the candy melts and insert them halfway into the cake balls.

4. Once the candy melts have fully set where the stick was inserted and the cake is back at room temperature, you are ready to dip the pops. Fully submerge the pops into the candy melts and tap off any excess.

5. While the pops are still wet, swirl the candy melts with a lollipop stick to add texture to the pop.

6. As the first coat of candy melts dries, prepare the Lifesaver mints. Draw four red bands on the tops and the sides of the mints with a red edible marker.

7. After the first coat of candy melts has set, dip a lollipop stick into the melted candy melts and drag it around the pop to add another textured layer.

8. While the candy melts are still wet, place the Lifesavers on top.

Octopus Cake Pops •••••••

Supplies

- Cake filling of your choice
- Purple candy melts
- Black candy melts
- White Sixlets
- Tic Tacs

Tools

- Digital scale
- Sheet pans
- Microwave-safe bowls
- Lollipop sticks
- Plastic bag

1. Begin by hand weighing the cake into one-ounce portions. Roll them into balls and set them aside on a sheet pan. Place in the fridge while you prepare the candy melts.

2. Melt the purple candy melts according to the directions indicated on the package.

3. Remove the cake balls from the fridge. Dip the sticks into the candy melts and insert them halfway into the cake balls. Dip the tips of six Tic Tacs into the candy melts and attach them around the base of the pop.

4. Once the candy melts have fully set and the cake is back at room temperature, you are ready to dip the pops. Fully submerge the pops into the candy melts and tap off any excess.

5. While still wet, place two Sixlets into the face of the pop for eyes. Place in a stand and allow to set.

6. Prepare the black candy melts in a small plastic bag, snip off the corner, and pipe black dots for the eyes as well as a dot for the mouth.

Shark Cake Pops • • • • • • • • • •

Supplies

- Cake filling of your choice
- Gray candy melts
- White candy melts
- Black candy melts
- Pink candy melts

Tools

- Digital scale
- Sheet pans
- Microwave-safe bowls
- Lollipop sticks
- Plastic bags
- 1½ x ¾ inch round cookie cutter

1. Begin by hand weighing the cake into one-ounce portions. Roll them into balls and set aside on a sheet pan. Place in the fridge while you prepare the candy melts and fins.

2. To create the fins, cut a crescent shape with a round cutter from a candy melt disk.

3. Melt the gray candy melts according to the directions indicated on the package.

4. Remove the cake from the fridge. Dip the sticks into the candy melts and insert them halfway into the cake. Attach a fin to the top of each pop.

5. Once the candy melts have fully set and the cake is back at room temperature, you are ready to dip the pops. Fully submerge the pops into the candy melts and tap off any excess. Place the pops into a stand and allow them to fully dry.

6. While the pops are drying, prepare the pink, black, and white candy melts in small plastic bags and cut off tips of the bags.

7. Using the pink melts, pipe the outline of the mouth and flood it. Allow to set. Pipe teeth around the mouth with slightly thick white candy melts. To achieve sharp teeth, pipe a dot onto each pop and drag it toward you. With the black melts, pipe on eyes and gills.

Starfish Cake Pops

Supplies

- Cake filling of your choice
- Yellow candy melts
- Jumbo star sprinkles
- Mini confetti sprinkles
- Sugar pearls
- Edible gold luster spray

Tools

- Sheet pans
- Microwave-safe bowls
- Lollipop sticks
- Toothpicks
- 2 x ¾ inch star cookie cutter

1. Stuff the cookie cutter with the cake mixture, using the palm of your hand to squeeze out any excess cake. Gently push the cake out of the cookie cutter. Soften the edges of the star by pushing down all sharp edges with your fingertips. Chilling your dough ahead of time makes this process easier.

2. Set them aside on a sheet pan and place in the fridge while you prepare the candy melts.

3. Melt the yellow candy melts according to the directions indicated on the package.

4. Remove the cake from the fridge. Dip the sticks into the candy melts while holding the cake with fingers, both on top and underneath, and insert sticks halfway into the cake.

5. In the center of the stars glue on a jumbo star sprinkle with the candy melts. Around each star attach five sugar pearls, and on each arm glue three mini confetti sprinkles. Allow the melts to set.

6. Once the candy melts have fully set and the cake is back at room temperature, you are ready to dip the pops. Fully submerge the pops into the candy melts and tap off any excess. Tap the pops with the back side facing you so that the candy melts do not pool up around the sprinkles. Place in a stand and allow them to fully set.

7. Once set, spray them with edible gold luster spray.

Note

If the cake starts to split and crack where the stick is inserted, rub candy melts along those lines for added support. Remember to use light-colored sprinkles, as any dark-colored sprinkles will show through the yellow candy melts.

METRIC AND IMPERIAL CONVERSIONS

(These conversions are rounded for convenience.)

Ingredient	Cups/Tablespoons/ Teaspoons	Ounces	Grams/Milliliters
Butter	1 cup=16 tablespoons= 2 sticks	8 ounces	230 grams
Cornstarch	1 tablespoon	0.3 ounce	8 grams
Flour, all-purpose	1 cup/1 tablespoon	4.5 ounces/0.3 ounce	125 grams/8 grams
Flour, whole wheat	1 cup	4 ounces	120 grams
Fruits or veggies, chopped	1 cup	5 to 7 ounces	145 to 200 grams
Fruits or veggies, pureed	1 cup	8.5 ounces	245 grams
Honey, maple syrup, or corn syrup	1 tablespoon	.75 ounce	20 grams
Liquids: cream, milk, water, or juice	1 cup	8 fluid ounces	240 ml
Salt	1 teaspoon	0.2 ounces	6 grams
Spices: cinnamon, cloves, ginger, or nutmeg (ground)	1 teaspoon	0.2 ounce	5 milliliters
Sugar, brown, firmly packed	1 cup	7 ounces	200 grams
Sugar, white	1 cup/1 tablespoon	7 ounces/0.5 ounce	200 grams/12.5 grams
Vanilla extract	1 teaspoon	0.2 ounce	4 grams

OVEN TEMPERATURES

Fahrenheit	Celcius	Gas Mark
225°	110°	$\frac{1}{4}$
250°	120°	$\frac{1}{2}$
275°	140°	1
300°	150°	2
325°	160°	3
350°	180°	4
375°	190°	5
400°	200°	6
425°	220"	7
450°	230°	8

Acknowledgments

Jessica Marin—Thank you for introducing me to cake pops. If you never threw that jewelry party and requested lady bug cake pops, none of this would have ever happened.

Grandpa—Although you didn't believe in cake pops at first, you were always there when needed without questions asked. Thanks for all those trips to pick up supplies and to ship orders.

Chef Dina Altieri—My first chef instructor who saw something special inside of me even when I didn't. Thank you for teaching me the importance of hard work and determination.

Annie Kelly—Thank you for being one of my first customers ever, who went above and beyond what anyone could ever ask for and helped out any way you could.

Marianna Dworak—Thank you for this wonderful opportunity, editing the book, and making the whole process very simple.

Index